T5-DHH-924

LOVEWORKS

COMING TO TERMS
WITH
INTIMACY *and* EQUALITY

Mary Ann Massey, ED. D.
and
Ronald W. Heilmann, M.S.W.

Jeremiah Press
Boca Raton, Florida

For Our Children
Michele, Suzanne, Nate and Ashley

May they choose partners who will
learn with them the meaning of
"intimate and equal"

and

For Jennifer
Who already has!

All clinical anecdotes are fictitious and not intended to represent specific situations or persons. Any similarities to real people's lives are merely coincidental.

© Copyright 1994 by Ronald W. Heilmann and Mary Ann Massey. All rights reserved.

ISBN: 1-883520-09-6
Library of Congress Catalog Number: 95-78908

Available From:

Ronald Heilmann, M.S.W.   Mary Ann Massey, Ed.D.
1940 Valley Drive   2170 Woodlands Way
Syracuse, NY 13207   Deerfield Beach, FL 33442
                800-949-4454

Published by:
Jeremiah Press, Inc.
Boca Raton, Florida
Printed and bound in the United States of America

CONTENTS

ABOUT THE AUTHORS

RONALD W. HEILMANN, DCSW, BCD

Ron received his M.S.W. from Indiana University in 1970. He is a Clinical Social Worker and Marriage and Family Therapist in private practice in Syracuse, New York, and immediate past president of the New York State Council on Divorce Mediation. He is Director of the Mediation Network of Syracuse which he founded in 1983; past facilitator for *Courage To Be* support group for the separated and divorced; team social worker for the Spina Bifida Clinic at Crouse Irving Memorial Hospital; lay speaker for Family Life Education and coordinator for *Children 1st* educational program for separating parents. He has been divorced and remarried to Jennifer, with whom he shares two children, Nate and Ashley.

MARY ANN MASSEY, ED.D.

Mary Ann is a Marriage and Family Therapist in private practice in Fort Lauderdale, Florida. She is also an adult educator, a public speaker, and a business consultant who is known for her expertise on women's issues, couples' communication, the divorcing stages, gender differences, and the process of change. Mary Ann has recently expanded her areas of specialization through doctoral studies to include the cutting edge field of Adult Educational Leadership. Her dissertation addressed the new management dynamics created by women sharing top executive positions with men. Divorced after nineteen years of marriage, Mary Ann has raised her two daughters, Michele and Suzanne, to adulthood as a single parent for the last ten years.

Bridging the Great Divide, a national seminar on gender differences, equality, and intimacy, has been presented many times by the authors during the past three years. If your organization is interested, please contact the authors at the addresses given in the front pages of this book.

ACKNOWLEDGMENTS

Five years ago, the Director of the North American Conference of Separated and Divorced Catholics invited us to create a conference on men and women. We had never met; we did not know each other's work; and we lived at opposite ends of the country. We listened to each other's audiotapes on various subjects, met in airports to discuss themes, and participated a year later in that conference which became a "happening" for all who attended, ourselves included. We thank all the men and women from that group who helped us give birth to this book.

We are grateful for the patience, generosity, and technical skill of our beloved assistant, Joyce, who worked with us evenings, weekends, and holidays to type and edit three drafts of this manuscript before it reached its final form. In addition, many colleagues, clients and friends read and critiqued our work, encouraging us to stay with the process. Note: Our anecdotal stories reflect typical issues and dialogues our clients have shared over many years. They are not, however, based on specific people or events.

We owe a large debt to Michael Miller whose incisive comments pushed us to speak boldly our beliefs about the journeys of men and women toward each other. This step, above all others, led us to walk the walk, even with each other.

We deeply appreciate the love of our families, their reassurance when we felt discouraged, their belief that we could accomplish our task, their willingness to set aside family time for us to work on the book, and their celebration with us over little successes. Mostly, we are grateful for the examples of loving that they are to us, for teaching us more about life on the real plane when we became too clinical, and for challenging us to trust the truth about them and ourselves.

We thank the special educators, therapists, and supervisors who have shaped our thoughts and our hearts over the years. In helping us understand and accept ourselves, they prepared us to see and appreciate more fully the uniqueness of others. This gift is immeasurable.

To our clients we owe our fondest thanks. The person who sits in the therapist's chair ultimately receives the composite benefit of all the hard work done by our clients. We are indebted to them for their sincere willingness to bring their honest selves to this endeavor and give us the privilege to work with them. What we have learned has come more from their struggles than our own. This book would not have been possible without their contributions.

Lastly, we thank the members of *The Courage To Be* group in Syracuse, New York, who, for nearly twenty years, have tended to the needs of those who have gone through divorce. From you and other support groups, we have come to write this book. Having witnessed your pain, been inspired by your hope and touched by your strength, we give back a little of what we have received.

INTRODUCTION

In 1945, World War II ended. Mankind had been saved from a cruel despot. The Allies had won. Soldiers returned and danced in the streets. Men and women went home and rejoiced in their reunion. During the next few years, record numbers of children were born.

These children grew up with a new piece of furniture in the living room, the TV. They watched Howdie Doodie, Flash Gordon, Superman, and The Mickey Mouse Club. They were inspired by "You Were There" and "The Twentieth Century." They were challenged to be "the leaders of the twenty-first century."

The youngsters went to school experiencing a strange mixture of events. They were given the polio vaccine at school to protect their lives; then, they periodically scrambled into hallways of the very same schools to practice covering their heads. They learned to read Geiger counters. In just a few years, those air raid exercises stopped. Many realized how futile it was to survive a nuclear war. These children were given much cause to reflect on their own lives.

Meanwhile, factories turned out wonderful automobiles to satisfy every budget. Kitchens were replenished with new, time-saving gadgets. Something was very right. Confidence in the American Way reached an all time high. There was no need to question anything. The proof was in the pudding. But the children of this generation of proud consumers faced some harsh realities. The bomb, beatniks, the Freedom Riders, the assassinations of the Kennedys, Malcolm X, and Martin Luther King shocked and confused them. They furrowed their brows and asked unanswerable questions. Then came Viet Nam.

In response to that war, flower children took to the streets, free love flourished, an assortment of drugs conjured psychedelic dreams, hippies railed against the status quo, and the anti-war movement grew. When the cause was lost, reflections on right and wrong abounded. Moral torment covered the land. Life's answers were no longer simple, clear, right, or wrong, even for the older generation.

By this time, the children had grown up and created their own adult worlds. Some made traditional families, some couples simply lived together, some raised children, some swore never to have children, some bore children out of wedlock, some sought illegal abortions.

Changes in the world at large now impacted the average family in the United States at its core. A word, once whispered rarely and shamefully in earlier decades, seeped into the culture: DIVORCE. Before long, the word and the pain it created became common. Other new expressions were also coined: Single Parenting, Blended Families, Test Tube Babies, Surrogate Mothers, and Sperm Banks, to name a few. Everyone wanted to know, "Why are there so many divorces?"

Why ARE there so many divorces?

Few people will argue that between one-third and one-half of all marriages now end in divorce. Some reports suggest by the year 2000 nearly half of all children will be living with only one biological parent. Of that half, most of those children will be living only with their mothers.

People often speculate on the root causes for divorce. Perhaps, it is too easy to divorce these days, they say. Although divorce has become more socially accepted, it is by no means "easy" to divorce. Couples kill each other's spirit in court daily, forfeiting thousands of dollars better spent on family care. The price of divorcing is high, indeed. Yet, men and women continue to leave each other in large numbers.

Others say the divorce rate is merely a reflection on a spoiled generation who wants everything their way. They acknowledge the "war between the sexes" yet cannot articulate what the war is all about. What *is* the tension between men and women which causes them to fight, too

viii

often to a bloody end? Why have communication failures between the sexes given rise to divorce now when earlier they did not? These questions beg answers.

Everyone agrees there is a communication problem. Professionals have toured the country for decades selling communication workshops to improve relationships, with marginal success. The war between the sexes has not abated; it is probably worse. Couples are, however, more able to clearly communicate their growing dissatisfactions with each other. Communicating is obviously not enough; nor is understanding. Men and women understand their complexities, even their differences, but they still do not know how to stabilize the intimate bond of partnership. What is at the root of this problem?

We, the authors of this book, believe we know the causes of divorce and have uncovered some answers. Through this manuscript we offer our insights to struggling couples. Divorcing is only one way to deal with disillusionment and despair.

This book is divided into three sections: **LOVE, HONOR, and CHERISH.** Each section demonstrates the transition of a couple from self-defeating beliefs and expectations about love's potential to a more enriching relationship. We use stories of everyday couples to convey the anguish and frustration embedded in the struggle to make a relationship work. Experiences particular to one couple, Tom and Julie, are related through much of the text to help the reader understand the transformative power embedded in a relationship based on equality. The intimacy generated in the process becomes tangible as Tom and Julie's stories unfold.

The first section, **LOVE,** describes the popular version of love that quickly brings to the reader's attention the pitfalls facing every couple. By the conclusion, no one is in love anymore. We begin to hear the agony of both partners as they wonder what has gone wrong.

The second section, **HONOR**, lifts the couple's agony to the level of a gut-wrenching scream. The apex of trouble is found in Chapter 6 where Tom and Julie rediscover each other's compassionate presence after many years. The remaining chapters in this section develop the primary thesis of the book: *Just when relationships appear to be at their worst, the partners find a new beginning ushered in by unexpected and unfamiliar intimacy.* Something realigns their relationship. It is "choice." By choosing a new basis for relationship, they learn to cherish the other in a way they never dreamed possible.

The final section, **CHERISH**, looks at the cost each partner pays for intimacy and equality. It develops a new kind of loving rooted in negotiation and "second best" choices and decisions. Finally, it describes the fruit of the labor for the couple and the ramifications for our society.

The dilemma of intimacy has been developed from the perspective of middle class heterosexual couples even though we believe the journey into intimacy is universal. We trust others will continue to articulate the process in ways that speak to the masses. In addition, the reader will notice some gender stereotypes. We appreciate that these will not consistently represent the experiences of all men and women and invite readers to take only what is personally useful with its transformative power into their homes.

Our choices reflect who we are and represent the couples' stories that have shaped our theories over the years. In a similar way, we owe a debt to personality theorists, master therapists, and countless other theoreticians and practitioners who have shaped our perspectives through our encounters with them and their work.

In the end, we rejoice and praise those couples who have struggled thus far to expand the potential of what is indeed possible for a loving relationship. We hope you will enjoy this book as much as we have enjoyed writing it.

SECTION I
LOVE

CHAPTER I
LOVE'S PARADOX

Love is a paradox. What one thinks will nurture love, destroys it. What some fear will end a love relationship can actually make it stronger. When love seems easy, it is risky. Holding onto love kills it; letting it go maintains it. Contradictions such as these abound when one takes on the task of looking at love between women and men.

To help you with this paradox and to help ourselves communicate something as elusive as facilitating love, we have decided to tell you a story. It is a collective tale of men and women in the late 1900's on the cusp of the year 2000. Since we, the authors, are both clinicians, our attempt is to create a therapeutic experience for you while you read. As in our therapy, this manuscript is a collection of "soft" science and a great deal of art. We do not have scientific data to back up our theories. We cannot prove anything to you. Yet, if what we say has some merit or some truth for you, we trust that you will find this work enormously helpful.

Because you have chosen to read this book, no doubt you too have been confronted by the paradox of love. You have tried your best to make love work. Despite your best intentions and the sincerity of your own love, the committed relationship within which love is supposed to flourish often withers like the roses of late summer. This is not your fault; it is bound to happen.

Most couples in a committed relationship try to preserve love by falling back on some old rules like, "Do unto others as you would have them do unto you." While it is heretical to challenge such time honored traditions, this idea, along with others, simply does not work for love. Instead, couples must relinquish all they have ever learned or concluded about love, if they intend to realize its power over a lifetime. The very thought confounds a rational person. It is like telling someone who is hungry that food will not satiate the appetite.

Most couples are honorable in their attempts to make love work. They do their best. They patiently listen to elders who hauntingly tell them that "love has its ups and downs." Oddly, the sages neglect to tell the young just what these ups and downs are, how long these times will last, and how to climb back up once they are down. This they are left to find out for themselves.

Since new lovers are left to their own devices, they apply the logical and intuitive rules absorbed via the culture. This is especially true when the road turns a little rocky. Lovers cling more tightly to these prescriptions when their relationship is threatened. It is like a skater who clings to the rail at the edge of an ice rink. For stability, he/she holds on more tightly, but by doing so misses the joy of skating.

When couples are in fear of relationship breakdown, they often panic, hold onto old rules, and scrutinize the partner's behaviors looking for solutions to the perceived problems of love. They use logic, make suggestions, and help their partners be good enough lovers. Despite such good intentions, the love erodes anyway. These attempts, at times, seem to hasten the deterioration.

Intuition and logic fail us when it comes to love. Although the internal relationship rules that guide men and women rarely match, they often share a common limitation: Discussing pain, dissatisfaction, and unhappiness on a deep personal level is avoided to preserve the relationship. Because partners hate to see the loved one upset, keeping pain, dissatisfaction, and unhappiness to one's self seems like the right choice. Holding back that which is troublesome is the intuitive choice. Holding back, holding on, and holding in continues until one partner snaps under the pressure in virtually fifty percent of marriages, and relationships worthy of a better break add to history's statistics.

The paradox of love must be addressed with another paradox: To preserve committed love relationships, couples need to decide to open the deeper parts of themselves, break out of secure old patterns, and let go of confining relationship rules—the exact opposite of what comes logically or intuitively. In doing so, they must threaten the relationship more, not less. This shift of thinking is enormous. It is like inviting the terrified skater to let go of the rail. This is not what someone in panic would choose. Now, let us add more substance to the problem. Suppose the skater is told the ice is cracking on the very spot where he/she stands. Everyone better move pronto or perish. Whether it feels safe or not, to let go of the rail is no longer an option given the new circumstances. Avoiding greater danger motivates a move. This is precisely what happens to couples in crisis. When more danger is realized by holding onto the old ways than venturing out into the unknown, a move becomes possible. The danger of remaining in the mold of a deteriorating relationship gives way to something new, yet threatening.

What will this new relationship be? How will it be established? What will protect it? On what can the lovers depend? These are all valid questions and worthy of answers, but no answers are possible until the skater lets go of the rail. Those already on the rink watching the action cajole, cheer, and sympathize with the wary skater. The same must be done for committed couples who need to embrace the unknown, not hold fast to a relationship deteriorating despite their best efforts to preserve it. They must be encouraged to go beyond the logical and the intuitive to the next step which is profoundly illogical and counter-intuitive.

The movement from a deteriorating relationship to fluidity and forward action is discontinuous. A definitive break with past actions is needed. A "leap of faith" best describes this task and is necessitated by the way the world of human relationships has evolved over the last century.

A CHANGING WORLD

Two major forces have been at work since the great depression, foreshadowing the need for marriages to change. The first has been a shift in the primary function of the family. The second force has been feminism.

3

The Family

The family used to be organized around the need to survive economically. While economics still plays a role in the life of the family, it is a less crucial factor. Since World War II we have become an affluent nation, perhaps wealthier than any other civilization since Adam and Eve. Even though family budgets are stressed, most adults have grown up in an era of relative wealth. The very fact that some women today can have children, raise them, and launch them into the world without men in their lives is proof that it is possible. This was unworkable before the world wars.

Prior to the last quarter of the Twentieth Century, a woman needed to find someone to take her and the children in after her husband died (or left). She had no other recourse. If perchance a man was willing to marry her, it was because the children were a potential asset to him. If a man with children lost his wife, he urgently needed a new partner or risk losing the children.

Today, there is time to choose new partners, make sure they are the right ones, and even develop prenuptial agreements to protect inheritance rights. The poorest of Americans still have options afforded them by our culture that have not existed before in human history.

Since economic survival is a lesser threat to the nuclear family than it used to be, the need for streamlining in families to guarantee economic production has gradually given way to a new alignment of the family. This new design is more suited to satisfying a higher level need, the realization of intimacy. Intimacy needs have always been part of family life, but a shift has occurred in priority. The push to experience intimacy has become paramount.

Commensurate with this evolution of the family, the new marriage between a man and a woman is less an economic relationship and more a union to experience intimacy. This new effort to realize human intimacy has changed drastically the expectations of marriage.

Feminism
The second factor affecting marriage became more obvious about twenty-five or thirty years ago. It became known as feminism. A commitment to the notion that men and women were of equal stature in all spheres of human experience gave direction and scope to the social movement. This revolutionary concept could only appear on the horizon once our economic survival was assured. Something entirely new dawned between men and women in North America in the 1960's. They yearned for intimacy and they were forced to deal with equality. They knew very little about either concept. They would learn at great price.

It is not surprising these two factors occurred simultaneously because they are interrelated. In order to realize human intimacy, equality is a prerequisite. This principle is clarified by observing the military which is organized rigidly in a vertical pyramid. Officers are continually reminded not to "fraternize with the troops" because to do so compromises one's authority in the system. Members of the military are encouraged only to have relationships with members of the same rank in order to preserve the integrity of the organization. More intimate relationships can best be realized with someone of equal stature! In the same way, for men and women to develop relationships that maximize intimacy, they must be equal. They must face each other on a horizontal axis, not stand one above the other, vertically unequal. Men and women are equal in value, equal in responsibility for care of the relationship, and equally capable of intimacy. Intimacy and equality are inextricably linked.

Relative wealth has given rise to the preeminence of intimacy in modern marriage; intimacy needs have created the conditions for equality. A problem emerges. Men and women do not know *how* to have an intimate, equal relationship. Additionally, they are not emotionally mature enough to do so. Most prior marriages, based on economic necessity, have been built upon vertical relationships exemplified by the illustration of the military. They functioned best when lines of authority were clear and uncompromising. Our ancestors have passed on a model of marriage perfected for functional purposes rather than for meeting intimacy needs. Today's couple must develop a new model to meet the demands of intimacy rather than function.

The relationship built upon equality to satisfy intimacy needs has many challenges. First of all, it is not as efficient for managing the ongoing functional business of family life, which does not disappear just because couples want more intimacy. Husbands and wives still have to raise children, provide for their care, and meet financial responsibilities. As they rearrange marriage to meet their intimacy needs, they will compromise the functional.

Think of the differences between businesses organized as sole proprietorships or as partnerships. No one argues with the CEO about how the business should be run. He or she makes the decisions, gives the orders, makes employees do what they may or may not want to do, and assumes full responsibility for what happens. The CEO is also compensated well for that responsibility.

In contrast, two equal partners running a business argue about what is in the company's best interest. They also must discuss nearly every decision in full until agreement is reached. Both must be simultaneously satisfied. The extra time and expanded effort renders this arrangement somewhat inefficient. Furthermore, it is less rewarding because the partners must share the profit; the net income for each partner will always be less than one run by a single CEO. On the up side, however, no individual will have to accept the weight of full responsibility; this will be shared.

The same tradeoffs exist for couples who move from a vertical marriage designed for functional efficiency to one horizontally designed to maximize intimate interaction. Business transactions will take longer, but no one person will have all the responsibility; and the possibility of intimacies will be enhanced. The couple is challenged to make the advantages outweigh the disadvantages.

A second and even more profound problem soon surfaces. Both men and women must become more emotionally mature in order to make an intimate and equal relationship work. Equally sharing the power, the responsibilities, and the profits demands a high level of emotional development not *required* in a vertical relationship. In equal relationships, a premium is placed upon negotiating skills, listening skills, and an absolute commitment to win/win outcomes. But modern men and women do not share a similar outlook on these skills because their genetic endowment and culturally defined roles give rise to differing definitions of negotiating, listening, and committing.

Much has been written lately about how different men and women are. Popular books have helped us realize that, although men and women are equal, this does not mean they are the same. Gender differences make sharing authority very difficult.

For example, men can be described as externally oriented. As their genitalia dictate, males are genetically and culturally predisposed to focus on the outside world. Their measure of value corresponds to their success or failure in the external world. Therefore, men are most preoccupied with their performance quotient and tend to measure their worthiness upon win/lose outcomes. They place a high value on being number one and measure themselves according to a vertical pecking order of power.

Women, on the other hand, as their genitalia suggest, are more internally focused. Also, because life comes from inside their bodies, they are poignantly aware of human connectedness. Deferring their own needs in service of nurturing and raising children and maintaining relationship connections organizes much of their value as females. This orientation is more horizontal than vertical.

Since men and women, due to their natures, behave and define themselves quite differently, these differences tend to become irreconcilable as men try to remain men and women try to remain women. Men will try to win as men win, talk as men talk, listen as men listen and negotiate as men negotiate. Women will try to maintain relationships as women do, listen as women listen, talk as women talk, and negotiate as women negotiate. Neither will be able to understand or appreciate the other, much less easily share power, authority and responsibility.

Moving to equality demands that a common language be used. Behaviors must also be received from some mutual standard, equally legitimate to the male and female point of view. When men and women try to develop a common language and new standards of behavior, they necessarily relinquish old traditional standards defining men as men and women as women. In so doing, they risk losing familiar and comfortable identity labels. This is often scary.

Defending rigidly defined sexual identities is at the bottom of all the arguments between men and women as they work out an intimate and equal relationship. On the one hand, they cling to their old identities, yet insist on sharing in all aspects of decision making in the new relationship. It is as if the two partners of this business each speak a different language, yet expect to function smoothly as a team! When they perceive the other does not understand, they simply talk louder in the still unrecognizable language. They innocently wonder why things degenerate no matter how hard they try. Hence, the paradox of love relationships: No matter how hard each tries to "fix" the relationship (a female fix or a male fix), it seems to disintegrate. The harder they try, the worse it becomes.

If men and women wish success in establishing equality in their marriages, they must redefine themselves as men and women. What makes a man, a "real man," and a woman, a "real woman" must undergo deep transformation. This is the emotional maturing that is required. A man will have to become mature enough to "feel like a man" even when he does not "win" an argument. A woman will have to become mature enough to "feel like a woman" to make her own self-care a priority.

Immaturity must be exposed if one is to understand what is happening to men and women on this intimate and equal journey. Men and women have not needed to stretch into such maturity before to maintain a relationship. This is a cultural change. It affects everyone. All must become mature enough to tolerate their own individuality within the context of a relationship; in other words, be able to stand alone with their respective sexual identities intact. This, too, is counter-intuitive and unfamiliar in a loving relationship.

When men and women come together in love, they do so to break a state of aloneness. They want to share a love, a life, a commitment, children, etc. Sharing love is the antidote to a life of aloneness once one leaves the family of origin. Pressure builds to stay connected to one's new family, but many cannot sustain the relationship despite their best efforts. The world is full of well-intentioned divorced people. These people did not plan to divorce on the day they married. Nearly every one of them planned to be together for the rest of their lives. What happened to them?

Stripping away the particulars of every situation, a common scenario looms: The couple cannot agree upon what is happening, and they cannot agree upon what to do about it. Each has his/her own version of the problem and the solution. It so happens they each seem to locate the problem in the other's behavior and insist that the other change so the problem will go away. "If only you would _____ ," one of the parties says, "I wouldn't have to _____ ." The other spouse repeats the statement using his/her own version of the problem. They each conclude that the behaviors perpetrated mean they are not loved by the other. They say, "If you really loved me, you would _____ ." The implication is, "Since you don't _____ , you must not love me."

Arguing and fighting attempts to convince the other to change his/her ways, so everything will work out. Rarely successful in this endeavor, spouses cannot even agree on a common reality: "You did!" "Did not!" "Did!" "Did not!"

As the spouses try to bridge their differences by establishing a common reality, they drive each other away, simply because normal healthy people generally do not readily surrender their own reality. This is especially true if they intend to share equally in power and authority. These people are already too strong to succumb to someone else's fancy. In the end, the spouses are married to their own points of view and forego their union because they cannot agree on anything. Since they cannot agree, they do not experience the intimacy of sharing which is supposed to accompany marriage. Like it or not, they are thrust out into the world alone again. In fact, it is now worse: It feels terrible to be more lonely in a marriage than to live alone. For this reason, many couples break up.

The intimate and equal marriage will only be established by two people who are mature enough for their respective realities to coexist independently from one another. In essence, each partner must be able to be alone with his or her reality, sometimes unconfirmed by the partner, and remain meaningfully involved in the relationship. For most men and women, this is an enormous step. It is excruciatingly painful to realize that the most important person in the world does not share one's own experience. The thought is almost incomprehensible! But it is real and immutable. Since no one's point of view has any greater credibility than the other's, couples must be prepared to live with a profound reality: In a relationship of intimacy and equality, each will at times be incredibly and profoundly alone. This is a disheartening paradox.

The remaining pages of this book will chronicle in a very personal way the typical struggle of well-intentioned men and women as they try to achieve intimacy in a relationship of equality. The reader will find how couples get in trouble, sink in the quicksand of marriage's paradox, and ultimately find a way out, but not before they have come many miles and learned quite a bit about themselves and their partner. Greater self-knowledge becomes the ground for greater intimacy, something sought for but arrived at in a very strange way.

We must look at the root drive for intimacy and find a way to let it surface. At least, the *desire* to experience intimacy seems to be mutual. Few men and women like being alone. That is why they marry. Yet, many face a blind alley of profound aloneness on the quest. What is wrong? *Is* something wrong?

The pages that follow will be the articulation of a process between a man and a woman, not a recipe or program, not a communication package, not just a description about how men and women are different. This book is an articulation of men and women's painful screams, the emotional convulsions which shake to the foundation their expectations of love. The shattering of idealized dreams leads to the sharing of real truth with each other. Then, in the mutuality of emotional nakedness, the war between the sexes ends.

The book is meant to be an encouraging voice. We believe most of you will learn to skate, swim, fly, and most of all, love, if you stay with us until the last page.

CHAPTER 2
THE SEXUAL DILEMMA

Couples are in trouble. Men and women, with the best of intentions, miss each other along life's way. Actually, it's worse. Couples find each other, invest great hope in each other to satisfy some unthought-through dream, powerfully disappoint each other, and then at least one of them gives up and goes away or shuts down. Sometimes they replace each other and sometimes they do not. It does not matter. Many couples are in real trouble.

Listen to some of the ways couples become stuck. They do not mean to get in trouble. They intend to love each other forever when they say "I do." Daily living burdens them and choices, made in loneliness, fear, or just pure temptation, affect them and others as well.

COUPLES IN TROUBLE

Jim and Pat have been married for fourteen years, the second marriage for both. Jim was attracted to Pat because of her outgoing, free-spirited ways. She knew how to have fun; he did not. He was a boring stick-in-the-mud at thirty-five. But he was bright, capable, prized at work, and respected in the community. Pat longed to have some goals and gain the same affirmation for her own talents, which Jim received without asking. Jim's grounded success in business intrigued her immensely. The attraction was strong for both; they married. After five years, he had learned to play, and she had entered the world of business management; they coasted. After ten years, they began to drift apart. Somewhere in time, Jim began an affair from which he could not break loose. He loved his wife and yet could not reach her. Obsessed with this other woman, he could not end the affair, nor could he marry her.

Postscript: This marriage ended in divorce. Jim worked his way into a corner. Pat left.

LOVEWORKS

Jenny is forty years old, the daughter of a minister, mother of five children, wife of a professional sales representative and not yet a mature woman. She looks and sounds like an adolescent. She loves her husband but is not "in love" with him. She values the security and friendship he offers, yet longs for something which is missing in her life. It may be sexual desire; it may be freedom; it may be love in another way. Jenny is not clear about what is missing but she is sure of her attraction to another woman in whose company she feels free to explore her secret sexual desires for the first time in her life.

Postscript: This marriage also ended in divorce, respect and friendship intact. The couple had been best friends but Jenny's secret struggles could not be solved from within the marriage.

Clint and Kristy have been married for twenty-one years. For five of the last six years, Clint had a clandestine affair. As the secret satisfaction waned, he felt confusion and loneliness. He wanted to end both relationships. When he heard himself tell a number of people, including his daughter, about the affair, he realized he wanted his wife to find out without his telling her himself. So he told her . . . and her fantasy marriage ended that day. He expected her to throw him out; he had already closed the door on the affair. Kristy didn't ask Clint to leave. She held him close to her and seduced him daily. She bought a sexy negligee and did whatever she thought might please him, desperately clinging to him, to her pride, to hope, to a shattered dream. She spent every waking moment with him outside of work and lived in fear of any attraction he had to another woman. Her nightmare was just beginning, not because Clint would be attracted to other women, but because she needed to face her own adequacy fears and learn more about love.

Kristy is a very beautiful woman, but does not know this. She spent the better part of the last year sexually focused to "keep" her husband connected to her. His affair was not about sex; it was not about her looks; it was not about his sexual satisfaction level with her. Clint's affair grew out of feeling trapped and emotionally clogged. He botched confrontations with his wife for fear of hurting her, longed for a friend who was his alone, and ached with loneliness. He did not know how to address any of it. Kristy's sexual solution was not about needing sex; it was not thought through at all. It was fear-based and fear-driven. When she was a little girl, she had been repeatedly molested by a neighbor who was good to her. Somehow, in the distorted and even painful sexual union, she felt wanted and cared about.

> *Postscript: Kristy and Clint have never been happier. Couples therapy has helped and their marriage is becoming intimate and equal. They are choosing to remain together, learning their responsibilities.*

Ashley and Bill have been married for twenty-eight years. He is a successful attorney, she a nurse and a strongly religious woman. She likes her husband and is afraid of him at the same time. When he's gruff, she feels like a little girl and works hard to temper his anger. She overprotects her children, suffers from migraine headaches, and avoids sex. Ashley not only avoids the physical relationship, she avoids talking about sex. She wishes marriage could work without it. She satisfies her husband when she realizes it is the shortest distance between two points. Even then, she does not bring her whole person to the experience. For twenty-eight years, they've endured the sore subject of sex.

> *Postscript: This marriage is in transition. The wife lets her husband in on life's problems. They talk now, and sex, surprisingly enough, is better.*

Pete and Cindy lived with each other for three years. Pete knew after one year that he did not love Cindy. He did not cheat on her, but he did plan to end the relationship . . . someday. He stayed two more years because he did not want to hurt her. He knew she really loved him and was counting on the relationship to become a marriage. He realized after he finally moved out, that he was afraid to be

14

alone. He had stayed with her to salve his own neediness, even though he did not love her. Hiding behind her fragility, he masked his own.

Postscript: Two years overdue, with much needless pain and suffering carried to its predictable conclusion, Pete left, of course.

Doris and David were married for twenty-five years. They had three children in college. David was a successful attorney in a prominent law firm, and Doris was quite well known in the community for her tremendous contributions of time and energy to civic concerns. They were the perfect couple in everyone's eyes. He was successful, and they adored each other.

Postscript: Why David killed himself remains a shock and mystery to everyone.

Michael and Betty dated for eight years, were engaged, married and then watched their relationship begin to deteriorate. Michael experienced sexual arousal difficulties with his wife, yet was easily aroused by other women. He concealed this for a year. When he risked the truth, the roof blew off their newly forming marriage. Obviously, Betty had known there were problems. She was beginning to think she was really unwanted when he told her about his problem. Preoccupied with her own raw reactions, Betty half heard Michael. Betrayal, fear, anger, confusion, and frustrated feelings of two years soared to the surface, blinding her from appreciating that the "problem" could now be worked out. Michael had withheld the underlying truth of his sexual struggles out of embarrassment, seeing his masculinity on the line; now his marriage was in question.

Postscript: Much talk, many fears, and a year later, they divorced. Their differences were too great.

Sex and love; love and sex. What is it all about anyway? So many life needs are acted out on the sexual plane. Numerous unnamed cravings are subsumed in the sexual connection. Lovers may hold desperately onto one person's sexual response to affirm their identities or enter into short term serial relationships for the same purpose. Sometimes, they avoid a one-on-one relationship, moving randomly from bed to bed. Sexual attraction becomes the avenue to acceptance. It can be consuming, competitive, fleeting, and always disappointing at some point.

What is sexual attraction? What makes us attractive to one person and not another? And why are men and women attracted to each other when it does not appear they want the same things from the exchange?

Sexuality is complex and problematic. It mixes current needs with those instilled from childhood memories of family, culture, and religion. It is spiced with innate gender specific tendencies and cultivated specifics. Attraction to the other sex is a powder keg!

Some of the sexual crises depicted in this chapter can be resolved in mutually satisfying ways. Knotty problems can become invitations to deepening intimacy.

What is entwined with our sexuality that can, on any given day, choke the life out of even good relationships? Men think they can never do enough to please, become angry and feel like the woman is controlling the show. The women go away believing men are selfish, convinced men only want one thing.

MEN'S SIDE OF THE STORY

It is true. Men do only want *one thing*. Despite their protestations, most men are preoccupied with the idea of "making it" with a woman. If men are truthful, they will admit that, for the most part, having sex with women gives organization and impetus to everything they do. Perhaps, this is why Freud, being a man, postulated the sexual drive as fundamental to all motivation.

However, there are good reasons why men protest when they hear women speak derogatorily about their sexual desires. There is a certain disdain in women's voices which negates the men's experience.

To gain a better understanding about the meaning of sex to a man, let us return to an earlier time in his life, a time when he realizes he is different from his mother. Somewhere after the age of two, it becomes clear to the male child he is biologically different from his mother.

All children, both male and female, go through an initial separation phase from mother establishing the child as a unique physical entity. However, the daughter remains aware of the sameness between herself and her mother, retaining a certain attachment to mother which ebbs and flows throughout life. This is not true for a son.

Knowing his differentness, the boy seems to say, "Well, if I'm different and if I'm separate, then I might as well get on with the business of growing up to be a man," and he does so with vigor. He looks around to identify with men and what they do. He knows he is distinct from the men, yet he recognizes the similarities, too. He would like to attach emotionally to the men if this were possible, but he cannot because he has not come from a man's body. While nurtured by his mother, he lacks the history of attachment to his father. The male child senses the difference without understanding it. He harbors a great sadness intuiting the choice between the security of an emotional connection to his mother masking his masculinity and fulfilling his masculine destiny by braving the uncertain world. The little boy sacrifices his emotional home and rootedness when he chooses to follow the course of becoming a man.

Later, sexual development presents males with another dilemma. The fact that women bear children (and men do not) strongly impacts the unfolding story of adult male sexuality. Women are reproductively connected generation to generation. They seem to be connected to the source of life itself through their procreative potential. Men do not have this universal rootedness to life. Theirs is a continual quest for connectedness in a world of separateness leaving them searching for emotional life, searching for meaning, searching for a fountain of psychic life-giving energy. A man's most profound connection to the source of emotional life is sexual union with a female.

A man sees a woman's life like a rosebush rooted in the earth. She receives direct nourishment from the soil and water from the depths. His own life seems like a cut flower placed in a vase. What will sustain the blossom? Even if he is lucky enough to find a vase with water in it, what soil will sustain him? His life, although prolonged by sexual attachment, seems limited and dependent, like the flower.

Connecting with a woman sexually continues as a man's preoccupation, even while he struggles to be productive in the world. Everything he does is motivated by his need and drive for a woman. She seems central to his well-being. Men do only want one thing.

Men are far more emotionally dependent on women than women are on men. They are dependent on women for this life-giving sexual connection. In their desperation, most men take the initiative. Waiting for a woman to initiate sex feels too vulnerable for these men. Men sense correctly that sex is less critical for women. Therefore, men conclude they must pursue women for sex, if their own needs are to be met adequately. Men only want one thing.

Men dread the perceived advantage they sense women have over them. Perhaps that is why men have been preoccupied with "keeping them in their place," as women express it. But men are not trying to keep women in their place as much as not wanting women to advance! Men hate their emotional vulnerability to women and feel controlled by women through sex. The one thing men need most is regulated by women. This reality puts women in control of men's lives in this crucial area. Men hate to be dependent; it threatens their masculinity which is largely based upon independence and autonomy. Dependency on women for the fulfillment of sexual needs is an untenable proposition for many men.

The more critical a man's need to mark his manhood, the more furious he becomes at women. This kind of man is likely to use sex as a weapon, taking sex on demand. Less aggressive men quietly hate women for controlling sex. Below the anger bubbles the fear of unwanted dependency.

In summation, men are jealous of women. Women are not vulnerable to men in the same way men are to them, envying women's connection to life. When men demand sex, they obscure the pain of loneliness and diminish the threat of women's control. Yes, men only want one thing.

WOMEN'S SIDE OF THE STORY

Women want one thing, too, only it is not the same as men. They want connection and closeness and value. They are ready to give men a large handicap in the game of love to these ends. A woman falls all over herself to please a man when she is in love. She will spend hours concocting a surprise, anticipating his need, preparing to give him pleasure in a thousand ways. He seems to respond to sex more than to the other things. That's okay . . . for a while. But it is not long before the value of pleasurable sex becomes entwined with the very life of the relationship. Men, it appears, need only to be satisfied sexually. Here the road divides.

As women become frustrated with men's ways, they fight over sex. Sex begins to feel like something taken from them, rather than something shared. It becomes one more thing they do for men, while getting little they deem important in return. Men simply do not do enough for the relationship! Women often experience their men not connected long enough or closely enough or fully enough. Therefore, they are often frustrated with men who promise much and deliver little. When they verbalize their needs, men label them controlling or unable to be pleased. Then women do not feel valued. They resort to complaining to each other. What's the sense of trying to talk to men? Men always do what they want anyway. Women then find it easy to keep secrets from men. It saves them from confrontations which seem to push men further away.

Women keep secrets about sex. Sometimes, women pretend they are aroused when, in fact, they are angry at their men and inwardly closed off. Other times, their non-arousal is related to natural hormonal shifts, fatigue, anxiety, or other distractions. If women do not take time to understand their own sexual desires, they can feel inadequate or imposed upon by men. Sometimes, they feel both. Their bodily responses remain an unexplored mystery while they

19

use their creative energies to cover up, pretend, and, ultimately, feel burdened by sex and by male sexual desire.

This is not a treatise on sexuality but rather a cameo of women's struggles and how they often compensate for what they do not understand in themselves or men. Many women do not understand their own sexual drive. Inwardly, they may be afraid of their own power. Outwardly, they are afraid of their partner's overt sexual power.

Sometimes women use sex for power because they know how hungry men can be and what they will do to satisfy their desires. Women know that men's desires are not like their own. Their desires, chameleon-like at times, submerge to satisfy men's needs directly, obfuscating for the moment any sense of their own. Women will endure much to serve the larger goals of establishing and guarding relationships, often without even realizing they are doing so.

Some women think mutual orgasm is important for men. They fake their own orgasms to protect men from feeling inadequate! Sometimes, women are afraid to make an orgasm personally important. To be responsible for personal sexual pleasure demands a shift from other-care to self-care. This is difficult when taking shelter behind other-care is a way of life. No wonder women think men are selfish and only want one thing.

Women enter into a sexual union to satisfy a deep longing for emotional and sometimes spiritual connection to men. Some women draw men to themselves through sex and hope to keep them connected through sex. It may appear women and men share the same desire in the sexual union. Passion levels may be mutual, yet, quite often for women, satisfaction is achieved primarily in the quality of the entire relationship. Sexual union is only part of the relationship and sometimes a vehicle to the "feeling good" aspects that may be temporarily missing.

Why do women keep secret their thoughts and feelings about sexual differences? Perhaps they think men will go away or not choose them at all if they admit sex does not have the same meaning for them. Asking directly for their own needs comes with great difficulty. Instead, women give *to* men what they want *from* men with the hope they will not have to ask.

Women give men a primary place in their worlds, and when all goes well, sometimes they may choose to defer to men's needs out of love. From women's perception, men do not seem to honor them in the same way for the same reasons. Women conclude that men only cater to them for sex. This leads women to believe they are sexual objects to men and nothing more. This perception has been at the core of many couples' arguments. To facilitate relationship building, women exhaust their energies talking about men, worrying about men, complaining about men, tending to men, and waiting for men to come home (emotionally and spiritually, as well as physically). Women continue to link sex and relationship care. When women think men are not co-equally caring of the relationship, they feel violated for their own sexual efforts. Fantasies of intimacy give way to anger.

Some married women use sex to reestablish broken lines of communication. When a spouse seems far away, the woman is scared. They make love and she feels better for a little while, until the brief tidbits of communion satisfy less and less her unquenchable desire for closeness with him. She pretends that sex is wonderful; when it loses its flavor, they both know, but neither speak up.

Some single women have been known to construe sexual sharing as deep level connection to men even if the relationships are brand new. They want to be chosen. They date; they see a light in a man's eye; the man calls back; a month goes by; the touch feels very nice. Something is happening. He clearly chooses to be with her. Sex is a way of expressing *something* for both of them. After a while, he feels uncomfortable with all the closeness she desires. After a while, she feels uncomfortable with his casualness about "them." Women do not open themselves up for a brief encounter without paying a huge price.

Today's sexual freedom may incline women to negate the reference to such a dated value. Indeed, many women participate in casual sexual encounters in which they truly do not think beyond the moment with their partners. Yet, most women lack the ability to sustain the focus of the sexual moment. Although they try to settle for less or go with the flow as long as they can, in the end, it is usually not enough without monogamy and permanence.

Sexual intercourse is a deep level connection that women enjoy predominately in an intimate relationship; relationship includes commitment to emotional connection; commitment honors the woman's need. This connection is more felt than labeled, more unconscious than known, and intrinsic to a woman's sharing of herself sexually. No matter how satisfying the pleasure of the moment may be, sex for women is, more often than not, about relationship, connection, continuity, and forever.

When women grow strong, many feel cheated in marriage, whether or not men cheat. Women work hard in therapy, in self-help groups, through reading, talking, musing and private struggling with the dilemma of how to fulfill their own and others' needs. They confer with other women, finding words for the cherishing that eludes them. Their secret pain smolders like a slow burning log.

For many, sexual adequacy takes years for women to cultivate. Their own ignorance and others' abuse of them must be reversed; sexual unfaithfulness must be challenged; and women's sexual ways, quite different from male response patterns, must be activated and taught to men. It takes time for women to claim their responses and desires as distinct and separate. They prepare differently for lovemaking. Arousal takes longer, and women need male touch, male presence, and words of love to open.

When men turn to other women, their partners feel inadequate, responsible, and guilty. The pain is exquisite. It takes a long time for women to realize the sexual indiscretions could not possibly be their fault. When they do, men's wanderings cannot be tolerated. Long stifled screams break loose into the atmosphere.

Women grow in and through the pain. As they come into maturity, articulating their sexual and other needs, they are saddened by men's ongoing sexual distractions. Women feel ready for relationships and find men less available than ever. It appears the more women connect to men, the more elusive men become. Men do not always turn to other women, but they do distance some. What is happening? What do men fear? This is quite confusing for women, especially when they want to love. Why do men walk away or choose another? Women know male sexual gratification is not object specific but they do not understand why.

One woman phrased the problem this way:

> *The sexual place inside us which we share with you men is special and offered in love. We open and close all our lives, intuitively protecting the sacredness of such a union which does not seem sacred for you. How devastating it is for us when another body is as desirable as ours. How utterly confusing when you can switch so quickly, so thoughtlessly, to another for pleasure. It is risky for us to open up to you. On what should we base our trust?*

Awareness like this prompts women to greater self-responsibility in relationships. Aware women reflect on their contributions to the sexual dilemma with their partners.

CHAPTER 3
NO ONE IN LOVE

Women want an emotional relationship in order to have sex.
Men want to have sex to have an emotional relationship.

The twofold dilemma of love is essentially this: Men and women want to be loved in the way they uniquely love; they want to *feel* being loved by the other the way they each *feel* their own loving. As a corollary, while it is possible to love and feel one's own love-feelings for the other, it is impossible to ever actually feel someone else's feelings of love. Men and women can only learn to recognize, receive, and give value to the other's expressions of love.

When Bob feels close to Mary and wants her to really receive his love, he will take her to the best gourmet restaurant in town hoping to end the evening with sex. When Mary wants to express her love-feelings, she wants to go away for the weekend, focus on "coupling," and spend lots of time together. Here is the problem. Mary does not feel loved at a gourmet restaurant while she is perennially dieting. Bob, from his side, feels uncomfortable with what feels like demands from Mary for too much closeness. Mary feels used and unappreciated for all she has to offer when Bob pushes for sex. Both Bob and Mary are unlikely to receive and give value to each other's love expressions. Instead, they will probably feel annoyed and devalued!

When men and women first fall in love, they give their respective loves to each other, that is, the love which is intrinsic to their natures. Because men tend to sexualize their love-feelings, the fabulous sex which is part of "being in love" is the expression of men's love for women. They offer women enormous amounts of attention as part of their fore-play of sexual love. For women, men's heightened attention to their many feelings and availability for good companion-ship and communication in the early stages all feel like expressions of love. Recognition of love as they know it ignites their interest in sex and they eagerly share themselves fully. They *feel* their own love-feelings for the other and receive from the other that which they *interpret* as love from the other. They *feel* their own feelings of being loved by the other but do not realize that their bases of feeling loved are significantly different.

The "in love" stage is particularly characterized by feelings of love, cued through reciprocal behaviors. Love-feelings abound. The freely given love behaviors are experienced by each as extraordinary affirmation, regard, and value which in turn give rise to *feelings* of being loved within each of the partners.

Feeling love for someone and the illusion of feeling their love in return seems to resolve (without even being requested) unconscious value questions: Am I a lovable man? Am I a lovable woman? Since we all leave home with some unanswered self-esteem questions, love seems to be the wild card that completes the hand. Falling in love exposes unconscious vulnerabilities for confirmation. Somehow, the sense of *feeling* loved brushes those very private places. Worst fears are laid to rest in the arms of the other. The security each longs for is suddenly within grasp and now containable.

Often people have not put words around a longing until they connect with someone who seems to activate it. When asked to define love, they say: "I don't know what love is, but I'll know it when I feel it." Or a young person may ask someone how they will know when they are in love and they are told: "You'll know when it happens."

Love feeds the soul. The affirmations embedded in falling in love are wondrously compelling. "I am loved! Wow!" Each new time someone falls in love, he/she experiences anew that "wow!" response. The very experience touches the roots of our beings. For a little while, people feel alive, powerful, abounding in energy, and accepting of all kinds of foibles and idiosyncrasies. The dislikes are not important now. Right now, what one feels when with the beloved is paramount. It is awesome!

LOVEWORKS

Julie met Tom after a relationship with a man who never had time for her. She had longed to find a man who could be stable enough in his life to be a companion. Tom found Julie while he was in a burnout period of life. He needed to play and he found a wonderful companion in Julie. Underneath the surface, in places each probably could not identify, they each needed root level affirmation. Julie needed to be seen and appreciated. Tom needed to feel adequate. They saw something in each other on the surface which felt like love. It was very real. They married on this magnificent wave of love-feelings. Under the surface, the daily affirmations bathed untended-to parts of them both. Their uncertain egos were reinforced, but at some point, the dynamics changed.

Julie and Tom probably would not be able to tell us when it happened, but looking back, several things stand out. Julie became pregnant; Tom returned his now energized self to advancement at work; Julie's sister moved to the same town; and Tom was asked to serve on a public service board. After the need for abundant affirmation had been gratified, Julie and Tom turned their attentions to the other loves in their lives. They went to their families, their jobs, her friends, his golf, school, art, the family computer, and various other middle class activities and hobbies.

Tom still loved Julie very much, but spent less time with her. Julie, still confident in Tom's love and reaffirmed by the early play times with Tom, went about preparing for the baby, helping her sister become oriented, and working part-time at the library.

As one or both of the lovers return to the real world of their "other loves" and become more involved in other life interests, two things happen. They experience a dilution of their love-feelings for the partner plus a lesser frequency of the affirmations coming from the partner. Julie lost some of Tom's attention and responsiveness to her areas of interest—the way she understands love. After the baby was born, Tom lost some of the playful sex life he and Julie had shared—the way he understands love.

These deficits are not even felt until one of them has a problem that triggers fear or pain. Perhaps, fear of learning about computers, getting laid off, breaking an arm, a car accident, or a big fight with a best friend changes the status quo. One partner needs some extra attention and turns to the other. Now the problem surfaces because the other is not as available as before.

If perchance, the couple shares interests, the dilution of love-feelings is less intense; one can be fed by shared interests for a little while. But, for most, the other's unfamiliar interests cement the original attraction; when the other continues life as usual, the hurting person feels alone. For such people, the reduction of affirming behaviors and the concomitant dilution of love-feelings is threatening.

To make matters worse, a partner who becomes emotionally needy (for any of the above reasons) often disapproves or resents the other for adding their other loves. They feel jealous. Normal life activities, on any given day, can become competing love interests. As life's complexity filters into the relationship, conflict potential escalates. The dilution of one's own love-feelings and the perceived erosion of the other's love-feelings (which are really only a lesser number of affirmations) seem to imply that the lovers are falling-out-of-love. Unfortunately, they compare the present situation with the early intensity of being "in love;" now, they feel deprived . . . for this they blame each other.

Tom and Julie drank from their over-
flowing cup of love until one day the cup was

27

almost empty. They tended to blame the emptiness somewhat on the other. Julie began to miss Tom who now worked long hours and had numerous commitments as a board chairperson. She felt less affirmed, saw less attention focused on her, and felt lonely inside. She indeed was jealous. Basically, she understood what Tom was doing and was very glad for him. But she could not shake the uneasy feelings inside. On the outside, she used her time fruitfully. She even found time to play with her sister and some of her friends at the library. She found new companions. Sex, however, left the top of her priority list.

Tom, preoccupied with work, did not notice Julie's activities for a while. When he had an unexpected day off and tried to find his companion, she was not available. This happened several times before Tom began to feel replaced, not desired, and lonely, too.

Two children, two promotions for Tom, and a full-time position for Julie later, they began to question each other's love. Each needed to feel love in that special way it once was. Good and understanding people that they are, they tried not to complain; but love-feelings continued to evaporate.

Unfortunately, "being-in-love" is the standard against which couples measure the viability of a love relationship. Each of the partners remembers how the sex used to be, how they catered to each other, how they felt affirmed in each other's eyes for almost everything they did. The dilution of love-feelings becomes subject to a misinterpretation: Love, not just the feelings of love, must be dwindling. Anxiety sets in. Their escalating insecurities and neediness set them up for more disappointment. The whirlpool is now in motion. The other's love is tested through the sieve of fear, interpreting normal behaviors in the worst possible light. (For instance, a new volunteer position means Tom does not love Julie anymore; fewer intimate moments tell Tom Julie is gone.) In panic, they turn back to the other to rekindle love-feelings.

> Tom suggests they plan a vacation to their honeymoon spot and Julie happily acquiesces. Tom knows he loves Julie and wants to feel her love for him again; Julie loves Tom and wants to feel his love for her.

The second honeymoon becomes a set-up for disaster. Remember, each cannot *feel* the other's love-feelings—but they *think* they can! They now scrutinize the other for signs of the other's love. They bring on this trip a dimension which was not important on the first honeymoon. They bring measuring sticks. Early on, no accounting was necessary. There was always enough love. Now, each begins to measure how the other loves with the only measuring stick available—their own unique, gender specific definitions of love. At the beginning of this section, we said that all of us want to be loved in the way we love. This becomes the dilemma of love.

> Tom and Julie have reached a critical point in their marriage. Julie wants Tom to make time to be with her and the children and to be interested in her activities. She tends to read his "busyness" as non interest. She has a full-time job, also, but it never interferes with spending time with loved ones. Only when Julie does not care a lot about people does she limit her time with them. Julie then infers that Tom's lack of attention is a sign that he does not care. When Julie loves, she very much wants to pour out that love with no measure. Tom has not been there to receive her loving gestures. Julie is scared.

29

LOVEWORKS

Tom is different from Julie. Spending time does not equal love for him. Tom measures love in terms of sexual desire and having fun. Although Tom has not mentioned it, he has been feeling somewhat concerned about their sexual life. He wonders whether or not Julie loves him anymore since she rarely seems physically to want him. Tom is always open to sex unless he does not like the person. If Julie does not appear ready for sex, he is scared and concludes she must not love him anymore.

Fuel is added to the fire. When a person cannot recognize the other's loving, he/she becomes angry. Each gives love and yet does not seem to receive love in return. Have they not given their love freely and in good faith to the other? Why is it not returned in a way each can understand? Anger ferments; arguments form a line of defense; "getting" becomes more important than "giving."

It is in this mixed emotion state that Tom and Julie go on their second honeymoon. They each bring a measuring stick. Tom wants to be desired sexually; Julie wants to walk hand-in-hand on the beach. Actually, Tom also wants to walk with Julie on the beach and Julie wants sex, but this is lost for the moment because their priorities are slightly different. *Each reads the other's greatest desire as a negation of the marriage contract to love.* The vacation does not satisfy either of their secret needs. They come home pleasant, having placated each other some, yet hurt, discouraged, and angry too. This anger does not go away as quickly as it did a number of years ago. Neither has done anything wrong but both feel unloved.

LOVEWORKS

The longer partners offer love and do not experience receiving love in return, the more angry they become. The more angry they become, the less they are able to feel love feelings. Often they lose altogether the feelings of love they shared at the start. Compounding the problem, old self-worth questions brought from their respective homes resurface.

Tom and Julie continue to back away from each other as they resume daily activities; they count on each other less to fill that special need place. They close off from the other to protect themselves from being hurt by the other. Where has love gone? Rage replaces anger.

Tom and Julie cannot see the forest through the trees right now. They cannot receive each other's still genuine presence. They fear rejection and live as though it is around the corner.

Now, no one's in love! At least, not Tom and Julie. They mix rage with despair. Julie feels a lot of pain and talks about it to friends. Tom buries his feelings in his work and contemplates an affair. Nothing has changed for the better in years. They have fallen-out-of-love-feelings, and they do not know what to do.

Tom and Julie hold onto their marriage for five more years. Each feels the burden of giving more than the other and receiving less. Oddly, each in his/her own way continues to love some with a love more comprehensive than how they feel in the moment. This very faint hint of pure love is mostly covered with pain. Hurt and rage simmer with brief respites of tenderness. The loneliness is profound and needs to be faced. Something has to happen. They cannot go on living like this.

LOVEWORKS

Love-feelings cannot sustain an intimate relationship, especially through times of discord, because lovers only know love-feelings based on their own terms. Honor, as an action, has bonding potential for couples in conflict, but it must be learned, developed, and chosen.

It is interesting that being in love does not lend itself to honor, but falling out of love does. The other is seen as separated from the self when love "fails." This feels like a violation. Ironically, it is a most positive happening. Only when love-feelings fail can couples treat each other with any consideration and/or esteem for their uniqueness.

The next three chapters focus on how to stay present in an intimate relationship when love-feelings are gone. These chapters form the glue necessary for modern marriages and are critical for Julie and Tom. They must substantiate their relationship on new abilities for which they have been ill-prepared. These proficiencies reflect honor. Three actions stand out:

1) Come to terms with the loss of the original love-feelings;

2) Grow in new respect for the differences which emerge in their world views, their behaviors, their needs, their pleasures, their values, and even their goals;

3) Learn to recognize the ways they still love each other.

LOVEWORKS

SECTION II
HONOR

CHAPTER 4
ESTRANGEMENT

Estrangement is crucial to developing intimacy. Most couples must face this extraordinary paradox and endure the loss of their dream partner before marriage can become a positive vehicle to intimacy.

No one relinquishes a dream partner without a fight. When couples even sense that their chosen other is not the special person they created him/her to be, the reality is too frightening to embrace. So they often spend years bypassing what they do not want to see. They excuse, minimize, endure, try to change, or cover up anything which threatens the love-feelings they carry in their hearts—until they cannot anymore. Truth smacks them in the face with a brutal force. A sense of forsakenness comes out of the shadows to envelop them. What do they do now?

The exposure of the other as limited in love is not the current problem. What gives weight to the overbearing sense of loss is the realization that the love which lives in their heads will probably not ever be satisfied with this partner. What does one do? When and with whom will this longing find rest? It is a terrible awakening! Each feels betrayed by the other in the light of truth. Love-feelings sink to the pit of one's stomach and fear surfaces to confuse the couple about what is happening. Tempting interruptive thoughts suggest doing almost anything to abate the fear. (Have an affair; leave; publicly devalue the other; hide out; spend all the money; eat; drink; etc., etc., etc.)

What is the fear really? Everyone has special words for it. For most, it is entwined with some unnamed hope left over from childhood that must still wait for satisfaction, be

33

placed on a new partner for satisfaction, or let go. The thought of letting the hope go prompts greater pain.

What needs to be let go? All married people need to let go of the fantasy hope they harbor for each other which is rooted in their individual love maps. New love rooted in adult mutuality can only be born in an atmosphere free from personal bias. We say this over and again on these pages. The problem with love maps is that they promote the illusion that the couple shares the same path to reestablish the old love-feelings. Wrong! This is the truth being exposed here. Men and women experience love differently. Couples are terrified of acknowledging different love maps, convinced as they are that this truth precludes ever finding love with this person. Wrong, again! They will only find love that highly regards another and is highly regarded by another after they stop sending each other treasure map clues the other does not pick up anyway. It is clear from Julie and Tom's dilemma that they have different maps.

Do not close the book now. You may think you know what happens next. Some of you do. Clearly, couples who do not hold their coupleness intact during the felt loss times know what happens next. The cherished love-feelings disappear and reasons for being married blur. When they cannot find their way in the fog, someone leaves. But love-feelings have to diminish and the marital contract needs to be rewritten. It is good the first contract is lost in the fog. This must happen. It is not necessarily the end of marriage, but the loss is tremendous.

These people feel utterly alone, the temporary result of facing the truth about differing love maps. It is one thing to feel lonely while living alone and unattached, but the pain of being in a relationship and feeling lonely is intolerable. Why stay married if their love needs are so different?

Panic-driven affairs and addictions of all kinds are sparked by an intense need to avoid feeling this lonely. Certainly, enduring this kind of forsakenness contradicts the meaning of marriage. This is not why couples marry. They marry never to be lonely again and to share the fruits of presumed similar love needs.

34

LOVEWORKS

Most people consider divorce at this point and a great many follow through. Vows, held over the other's head like a Damocles sword, become themselves weapons: "You promised to love, honor, and cherish me. You owe me! You'd better shape up." Couples struggle with why they stay together. No one feels loved; limp attempts to give love are rebuffed or diminished. Forsakenness sets in to fuel already distorted thinking: The relationship must have been a mistake. Attraction to another must mean the end of love; feel-good love is gone, so the marriage is over, time to move on and hopefully feel better again.

Julie and Tom have reached this point and so have some of their friends: Tim and Joan, and Ted and Janet. (To give an example of the options available to Julie and Tom, the authors divide the couple into three mythical parts.)

THE DIVORCE OPTION

Tim and Joan decided to divorce. They did not want to work at getting their needs met through the other any longer. They found lawyers and began the arduous process. It was a relief to admit the relationship was beyond repair. Neither had any more enduring energy, anyway. So they gave way to expressing their respective angers and raged at each other, using the divorce as a catalyst to let the other know just how much they were hurt.

In the early stages of divorcing, Tim and Joan felt no hostility. The decision had been mutual. But distrust, fed by insecurity, ignited their worst fears. Simple behaviors, such as Tim's returning to the house while Joan was away to pick up some personal items, turned against them both. Joan, concluding that Tim would take everything not nailed down, changed the locks; Tim, interpreting this action as Joan's taking possession of everything, staged a break-in; then Joan obtained an order of protection. Within three weeks, hostility escalated. The children were sent to therapy.

Two and a half years later, Tim and Joan divorced, but the war continued. They thought the divorce would end their relationship, but care of children and family business still enjoined their worlds. More collective decisions were necessary now than when they were married! This they had not counted on. War-torn and battle-scarred by reality's blows, they fought on, each trying to find peace apart.

THE ENDURANCE OPTION

Ted and Janet decided not to divorce. As a matter of fact, they never even discussed it. Janet gave up trying to turn Ted's attention to family matters and her own needs. If she could not convince Ted to love her more, she would just take solace in the children, put her shoulder to the wheel and do the best she could alone. Ted knew something was wrong but could never quite find the time to figure it all out. He was very busy, rarely at home, and thankful Janet did not harp on him like some of his friends' wives. When she asked for separate bedrooms, he agreed. The move was a response to her depression.

Ted involved himself even more in the community, added business travel to his schedule, and had brief, secret affairs while away. When home, he drank more heavily. Janet was sick often, went to bed early, and lost herself in books. Otherwise, the family shared meals regularly; the children had fun times with each parent; and the couple went to social gatherings when expected. Living lives of quiet desperation, they passed off their pain as a necessary consequence of staying together for the children.

Janet and Ted held all the pieces together, providing their children an intact family home. They settled in for the long haul and actually felt proud of what they accomplished. On their fiftieth wedding anniversary they held hands and smiled brightly as they cut the cake their children had made for them.

THE WORK-IT-OUT OPTION

Tom and Julie had a much more difficult time, mostly because they could not agree to divorce and they absolutely could not agree to shut down and live like strangers. We pick up their story at the worst point in their history:

LOVEWORKS

After returning from the second honeymoon, their relationship deteriorated further. The vacation had not rekindled the love-feelings as they had hoped and did not return security to their marriage. The experience backfired, reaffirming instead the emptiness they each feared. The love-feelings could not be revived.

Disappointed and angry, Tom and Julie nipped at each other in fights which led nowhere, each sparring match terminating with the same plaintive cries: "Tom, you are selfish, self-centered, and do not care about me anymore. You let me manage the household, the kids, school, repairs, bills, and my own life. You do not even know what I am interested in anymore. You stopped telling me about your life a long time ago, and you never touch me unless you want sex."

Tom would counter with: "Julie, I do not know what you are talking about. I come home every night, I work hard, and I provide for our family. What more do you want from me? I never have any time for myself. When I take a little time to play golf, you remind me of a thousand things the kids need, we need, or the dog needs. I cannot handle it anymore. You are very unrealistic in your expectations of me. And what's wrong with my wanting to make love with you? You pull away from me all the time. It makes me feel terrible! If you do not want me, I'll find someone else who does!"

Tom always rallied after one of these outbursts. He did try to keep Julie happy and would unravel when, despite his efforts, she became angry with him again. Julie rallied too and endured a little longer the hard task of running a family. She secretly hoped he

would bring home flowers or plan a date,
anything which would let her feel special to
him. When no special treatment ensued, she
became angry at almost anything, deliberately
turning away from the only thing Tom
pursued, sex. Their sex life in the pits, Tom
could not figure out why he stayed. He felt
unappreciated and very tired. He hated his
angry explosions, not liking the violent, abu-
sive man he saw in the mirror. He hated Julie
for not understanding him better. He hated
life in general.

Julie had been seeing a therapist for
quite some time but had not told Tom. When
she finally asked him to join her for a ses-
sion, both knew they were in serious trouble.
They even talked about separation and entered
into an eerie quietness that terrified them
both. Forsakenness mixed with sadness and
remorse. Fatigue diminished hope. Neither
spoke the divorce word, yet each contemplated it regularly.

Tim and Joan, Ted and Janet, and Tom and Julie
have all experienced forsakenness and lived out estrangement. Tim and Joan divorced; Ted and Janet remained
together but lived separate lives; Tom and Julie fought for
the marriage created in their own separate heads until anger
and loss brought them to despair. Each of these people felt
like they no longer really knew their partners. The other was
not the person they had married so long ago and they barely
recognized themselves. The estrangements were profound
and devastating.

Tom and Julie are on the brink of new life but they
do not know it. Each has to come to terms with a profound
disillusionment.

CHAPTER 5
DISILLUSIONMENT

THE MAN'S EXPERIENCE
The "I" of the Hurricane

One Friday afternoon while driving home from work in a light rain, Tom noticed a building being demolished in an old section of town. Unconsciously, he pulled off the road to watch. Between the intermittent wipers he studied the unsightly mess. The wet broken pieces of stone reminded him of the devastation wrought by a recent hurricane. Pondering this rubble, his own life came into focus. "My God," he thought, "my life has been smacked by hurricane-like winds and I am personally sitting in the middle of the eye."

The eye of a hurricane is a very strange place, mused Tom; it's a temporary haven of absolute calm. The worst turmoil of nature precedes and follows its silence, ushered in by winds strong enough to drive straw through a telephone pole. Landscapes are ravaged and torrents of rain flood the streets, floating cars as if they were row boats. In the blink of an eye, destructive winds dismantle all that had been carefully constructed and treasured. Tom grimaces. Such winds of anger have already damaged his life and family and still loom threatening on the horizon.

Tom seems mesmerized by the image of a hurricane's destruction: Houses, the work of man's hand, blow off their foundations and shred like paper. Giant trees, meant to last forever, uproot like weeds pulled from the garden. Chaos and confusion reign.

Suddenly, calmness descends; the sun shines in the blue sky above the eye for a short period of time. Droplets of water glisten on bright green grass. Everything glows with a freshly washed appearance. Nothing moves. Silence prevails. The spirit of God seems to hang in the air. The visible wreckage is the only disturber of a magnificent peace.

As Tom slumps behind the wheel of his parked car, he realizes his life too has been tossed around. For the moment, though, there seems to be a reprieve. Funny how an uneasy peace permeates this moment for Tom who sits in the debris of yesterday's turbulence and anticipates tomorrow's ominous storm watch. Silently, tears roll down Tom's face.

"How can stillness follow such terrifying violence? Why, right in the center of a hurricane, does nothing move?" Tom says to the windshield. The eye stands in stark contrast to the surrounding fury. Tom knows he has had a personal reprieve; the storm is far from over.

From his car, Tom surveys the wreckage and inventories what remains of his life. His neighbors are gone. Tim and Joan now live separately. Ted and Janet are together but are sad and not much fun to be around. His work is unfulfilling. He is tired of the bar scene, the gym, and watching TV. He and Julie are really on the ropes. "Without her, life will be very different, but it is too painful to go on with her as things stand," Tom reflects. He quivers inside at the thought.

Tom encounters his own frailty in this quiet place. It feels as though his life is in the balance; it feels like he is coming apart just like the building in front of him. Partly, Tom is already dead. His wife and children are still in sight but they are not really connected to him. Slumped in his car, more alone than ever, a disquieting peace enters his being. "What is happening to me?" Tom sighs.

His mind wanders back to childhood and the loneliness which began very early in his life. He used to play in the woods by himself. He knew even then that he was separate from the masses. Maybe the early awareness of his own separateness gave birth to this loneliness that he still harbors. His mind focuses on his friend Rudy, and he smiles. Luckily for him, Rudy's family moved next door just before he entered school. From that point on, Rudy, then later Richie, Dale and Davey helped him not feel so alone. He enjoyed their companionship for six or seven years. Time and school, different interests, and finally girls split them up. By high school, Tom felt very much alone again. He still had many friends and acquaintances, but no one touched an odd separate part of him, isolated somewhere in his body; this self had an appetite which little satisfied.

A sudden blast of a car horn startles Tom out of his reflections. He has been lost in his painful memories. "How come these are the same feelings tearing at me now?" Tom grimaces. This bothers him. The rain has intensified since he first pulled off the road; automatically, he turns up the wipers. "Dad, why do I always think of you at these times?" he said to the air. The loneliness usually leads Tom to think about his late father, who was a good and caring man and a significant figure in his life.

Tom's father was rarely home. Business commitments occupied a lot of his time. Tom searches his mind but remembers only three vivid memories of seeing his father at work in the eighteen years they lived together.

Tom was eight when he first visited his father's job. His father took him to the factory where he was a supervisor and let Tom ride with him on the forklift. Tom burst with pride while sitting on his father's lap and driving the fork lift. The memory touches him even now.

Later that day, Tom's father taught him to look through a peephole on the side of a giant kiln that fired the ceramic tips of the spark plugs produced in this factory. Then he taught Tom to use an instrument which, when looked through, revealed two brightly colored bars, one reflecting the heat of the kiln; the other's color was adjusted by a dial on the side of the instrument. Tom learned to match the two colors to take the temperature of the kiln with the instrument.

The second time Tom visited the plant his father sent him off to take the temperature of the kiln by himself, which, of course, he did. His father checked the reading with one located on a separate monitoring machine in his office and told Tom his reading was exactly right. Tom burst his little buttons with pride. He was his father's son; he could do what his father did. The joy of this memory was suddenly cut short with the realization that he never went back to his father's factory again. That which excited him most never reoccurred. Loneliness engulfs him in the silence of the car.

LOVEWORKS

Tom has no other memories of his dad at work. But he has an outstanding one from his scout days. One weekend, Tom's father went on an overnight camping trip with him when he was in Boy Scouts. Dad slept in the station wagon because he arrived late from work. Tom slept in the tent with the other boys, knowing his father was close by. He remembers it as if it were yesterday. Although Tom did not see his father very much that night or even the following day, he could always feel his presence. His father was there in the background, giving comfort and reassurance, even though Tom was with the scouts.

"Where is that feeling now?" Tom wonders. He misses his dad a lot sometimes; he was not able to be around him enough when he was alive. Tom ironically realizes that he is now doing what his own father had done. He is working himself to death to provide for his family. Tom sees himself doing what he is supposed to do as a man and as a father, but missing his own children, too. This realization amplifies his internal ache.

"Has there ever been a time when this loneliness left center stage?" Tom says to the empty seat next to him. "Yes!" he answers himself. It happened when he met Julie. She filled that emptiness for him. Julie gave value to Tom's life and his choices. Even now he does all he does to gain her love, the only medicine that numbs the pain. When they are physically intimate, he feels renewed.

Here is the heart of the matter for Tom. He has been doing everything in his power to make Julie happy; yet, she is never satisfied with him. Tom hoped that by marrying her, working hard, and loving her, he would maintain her affections and fill that chronic void in his soul.

Tom now realizes that being number one in Julie's eyes took precedence over his recent career struggle. He always feels vulnerable at work. Although he has a good management job, there is little job security these days. He cannot pin his hopes for fulfillment on the insecurities of his career. Julie represents his only real remedy for the pain. She always has and always will be his bottom line. This is why he is so damn mad at her. His life depends on her love

42

and yet all he receives from her right now is negativity. By rejecting him sexually she deprives him of his main cure for the loneliness. He has been furious with Julie and terrified too. If she goes away, he may be stuck with the pain forever. He cannot count on her to help him anymore. With this last awareness, Tom rummages through the glove compartment for a tissue. Where the hell are they, anyway?

Tom has smashed the structure of their marriage with the wrecking ball of his anger. He has pushed his haunting, lonely ache down and converted it into rage. He is holding Julie responsible for his unhappiness even though he had his pain long before he met Julie. It seems logical to blame Julie, but he also knows it's unfair. She took away his pain before; why cannot she continue to do so now? Tom's constant anger has alienated her more and more. He unwittingly contributes to his own loneliness and eventual demise. He finds himself destroying everything which is really important to him in an attempt to avoid this blasted internal ache.

Tom's anguish is broken by the sound of the wrecking ball slamming into the vacant building one more time. Although Tom has been thinking about how mad he has been with Julie, he is surprised to realize he is not angry with her right now. This calm within the hurricane is intriguing. The peace he now feels reminds him of the relief that enveloped him when he found Julie the first time. She made him feel important and wanted. When did this go away?

"Katie!" Tom said out loud. "Life changed dramatically for me when our little Katie was born." Deep in his heart, Tom knows he lost Julie when Katie was born. The Julie who had been there for him no longer held him as her priority; Katie was more important. This secretly shattered Tom, but he was too ashamed to admit it. He kept this secret to himself, feeling on the outside of a love triangle within his own home. Why did it look like Julie found a lot more fulfillment with Katie than she did with him? She seemed complete as a woman in a way he never felt as a man. He loved Katie just as much as Julie. Yet, he could not understand why he felt so bothered by the birth. It seems everything has been going down hill since.

LOVEWORKS

The wipers on the windshield disturb Tom this time.
He has been lost in the stillness of his life space. Now, he's
talking out loud, tears still running down his cheeks.

Okay! I quit! Julie is not my answer
to happiness. I cannot continue to find life's
solution in pleasing her. Nor can I avoid
dealing with our relationship by hiding in
work. The costs have been enormous emotionally. The more I try to demonstrate to
Julie I care about us and love her in the only
way I know, the more distant we become.
Clearly, our sex life is getting worse, not better. In this honest moment, I can see that I
control my anxiety by attempting to connect
with her physically. When I have her, I feel
okay for a while, but never for long. That
damn "dis-ease" returns. The more I try to
control my life, the more out of hand it
becomes.

I become a raging maniac if I cannot
have sex. When I am not pursuing her, I
find myself chasing after some one else,
either in my head or in reality. If I leave
Julie, I will lose the most important piece of
my life; yet, if I stay and keep doing what I
am doing, I will destroy her, myself and the
children in the process. Each way, I lose.

I am tired. I've been a good provider
to my family. That has to be worth something. I took care of them all, but who's taking care of me in the way I need? Maybe
what I need will never come. That's hard to
swallow. Why am I married then?

I guess I will have to care for myself.
I will have to count on myself alone and find
some new strength somewhere. Where? It
was supposed to come from Julie.

LOVEWORKS

Exhaustion is not the only price I have paid for trying to work things out with Julie. I lost track of my children in the preoccupation with my ache. While seeking my own gratification, my children have grown up. How did I lose so much of my life? My son played high school baseball without me in the bleachers. My daughter, my innocent little girl, is already dating and I am afraid for her. God, what damage have I wrought by not being more present for them? I fear they wrote me off a long time ago when I was not looking. They are good kids, my kids, but I hardly know them now. I cannot even remember what we did together.

I have depleted my resources with a multitude of distractions and have seriously jeopardized my health. I have risked addiction and worse, all in the effort to make my mark in the world and ease my agitation.

What the hell is this uneasiness that haunts me? Why am I so restless? Why does nothing soothe the pain? What is the storm in my own soul? I must know. The hole in my soul has been here for so long I cannot remember a time when it was not. Wait. Yes, the Boy Scout camping trip! Knowing my father was in the back of the station wagon while I slept in the tent gave me peace and comfort.

Why do I remember this event so clearly? What is it about his presence, although unseen, that gave me the strength and will to continue growing up and feeling content? Perhaps this is a clue to the source of the new strength I seek. Father, I am all out of resources again. I need help.

I have decisions to make. I am no longer sure of anything. I do not feel like a real man. I tried to be a winner. Instead, I have failed. Everything I have built has disintegrated. Oddly, trying to win has resulted in loss.

My life requires regrouping but I do not trust myself to do this alone. If I do not find some help, I will surely perish. Something more is needed than my own abilities, something more than a good woman, something more than riches. I need to hold onto the peace in the center of this storm.

Now is the time to find shelter for the second half of the storm; time to gather my wife, if she'll come, my children, the dog, and the cat; time to return to the shell of my home and see what can be done. God help us.

Tom put the car into gear and drove home. Tom is now dead in the water! Yet, on a feeling level, he is more alive than he has ever felt in his life. True, most of his feeling life is pain, but now the pain makes him feel very much alive. The storm of his life has not killed him and he can look back on the rubble, determined, with God's help, to do more than try to change Julie or the way she sees him. Tom decides to be true to himself no matter what. Meanwhile, Julie is also assessing her life in a way which shatters her dream-based world forever.

THE WOMAN'S EXPERIENCE
The Waiting Room
Halfway through life, women give power to nagging questions which they keep at bay for years. Feeling empty, used, and left out, insights surface in them that shake them to the core. Women, who use their energies primarily for the care of others, realize their emptiness will not be filled by their jobs, their husbands, or even their children on whom they lean for much compensating comfort. It is a devastating awakening.

In earlier years, questions like, "When will it be my turn?", "When will my family take care of me like I take care of them?" and "Why does my spouse still buy daisies when I've always loved gardenias?" were dismissed as selfish. Women consoled themselves in being needed, in feeling responsible for the family's needs, and in enjoying others' pleasure when special niceties were done for them. They waited for their partners to "get it," to do in like manner to them, but many never did.

As women age (and maybe mature), they tire of caring for others when it now seems too much at their own expense. They begin to "get it" themselves. Many realize they have waited unconsciously to be loved back as they love. It dawns on them that this probably will not happen. This insight is the beginning of new life for them. It feels awful and some couples do not survive women's awakenings . . . their coming out of their private waiting rooms.

Julie is on that personal threshold and very angry at Tom. It is not uncommon for women to focus their anger at this juncture on the men they love and possibly even on men in general.

Julie's escalation of discontent in her marriage coincides with the birth of her sister's second child. Maggie asks Julie to be her substitute coach for the birth. Julie jumps at the opportunity. The intersection of the two waiting rooms sparks an internal dialogue during the long night in the hospital.

While entering the hospital, Julie feels pulled to reflect on her own history and the painful waitings which marked her own life. She remembers how "loving" meant tending to everyone's needs, trying to make them happy, feeling satisfied when those she loved were content, and feeling great unrest when those she loved were in pain. She frowns thinking how often she deferred her own needs when any of the family needed her.

"I've changed so much over the years," she almost said out loud, unhappy memories causing her to grimace. "No more! I cannot wait any longer for my turn." Even thinking the words rekindles the fear, anger, and confusion she traditionally tucked away from her awareness. "I have been married to waiting and I hate it! Loving and waiting have made me a martyr. Tom doesn't seem to have this problem. How come I do?"

Outwardly, Julie talks to Maggie and tends to her needs; inwardly, her thoughts move along a totally different track. "I feel good about myself when all the people I love are content. I can't separate myself from them. When Tom and the kids are happy, it makes my day. When they are upset, I absorb their pain, too. I don't think Tom is like me. I'm not sure he even notices when one of us is having a bad day. When I love, I always notice others' feelings. Not Tom. I just don't understand! I've waited and waited for him to show *some* sensitivity to my mood shifts, but his head must be in a cloud. It's no fun!" The doctor interrupts Julie's meditation: "Five centimeters!"

"How prevalent waiting is in women's stories," Julie continues inwardly. "Women wait for periods and pregnancies, for wars to end, for children to grow, for menstruation to begin . . . and then end, for chores to be finished, and for time to focus on self. And women have believed that they are good because they wait well. Maybe that is my problem. I've confused waiting in all these ways with loving! And loving is confused with self-sacrificing. Many of us women are tireless, it seems, in tending to others . . . until we become angry. I have paid dearly for placing myself last," Julie realized, "all the while waiting for someone else to put me first!"

Julie is oblivious to ongoing hospital bustle. She contemplates other insights which caused her to face how much waiting weighed her down over the years.

She had created a compound dilemma: First, she waited in vain for Tom to give his encouragement as she entered the business world. Julie reflected on how several years ago she waited for Tom to support her efforts to be a wage earner. She waited and waited for his blessing, but it never came. At best he gave guarded assent and mostly seemed irritated by all the schedule adjustments necessitated by her taking her new full-time library job.

Secondly, she has waited, even to this moment, for Tom to love her enough or even a little in a way that feels right. Previously making her happiness contingent on Tom's approval of her in business, she has now additionally deprived herself of value by waiting for Tom's love at home.

The frequency of contractions draws everyone's attention. "Eight centimeters," the doctor says with a smile. Julie smiles, too, knowing this waiting, at least, is almost over. "I've stopped waiting for Tom to compliment me on my library job. I'm better than I've ever been in many ways. I really have stopped waiting for Tom to make my life meaningful. But what has it gotten me?"

Julie is amazed at how tenaciously she had counted on Tom for meaning to her life . . . and how angry she had been when she stopped waiting, as though he had failed her. It took a while for her to realize that Tom was not a bad guy because she had to live her own life. "That's when I made a lot of changes," Julie thought, nearly speaking out loud. "But I am still unhappy even though I like myself better. I still wait for love to be right with Tom and wonder if it ever can be?"

This situation plagues many women. No matter how liberated they become, they still wait for men's love. Women wait for men to participate in relationships as they do! They wait for men to understand the nature of relationships and to be as attentive to others' needs as most women are. At least, Julie did.

Waiting-for-love has nearly defeated Julie. Her present disillusionment is one of the few feelings powerful enough to dissipate her loyalty to Tom. "Why am I waiting so long?" has become the question which leads Julie to face her own needs and address the limitations in her marriage.

Maggie calls Julie's name, aware that Julie is mentally distracted. Julie focuses on her sister for a few minutes, wiping her brow and breathing with her, but her private thoughts are compelling. She slips back into them.

Julie realizes, "I am in my own private waiting room, and I do not know how to leave it! In addition, Julie is very, very angry and has avoided acknowledging it.

LOVEWORKS

Like Julie, many women avoid knowing they still wait for love. They may say they give up on a relationship, that they don't care anymore, but women lie to themselves. They do not let go of loved ones easily, and they especially do not let go of the love they have waited a lifetime for. They still wait when they say they are not waiting—for the fulfillment of their hearts' desires with men, for their children to grow up and validate their mothering, and for appreciation of all their hard work. They wait and do not even know they are still waiting. That is the tragedy. Women often know only in retrospect how much waiting they have endured.

While waiting for her sister's labor to end, Julie remembers an event which typified her waiting mentality. One birthday she had expected to be taken on a cruise. Julie waited and waited. Then she concluded that because it was the middle of the week, Tom must have planned the trip for the weekend to make it really special. The weekend came and went, too, with no cruise! Two weeks went by before Julie blew up at Tom. Last year he had told her he wanted to do something special for her fortieth birthday and she let him know that a cruise would be special. She waited a whole year for that cruise. He gave her diamond studs instead and she didn't feel loved. Julie becomes angry just thinking about this incident. "He forgot! He told me he forgot I ever said anything about a cruise. I had sacrificed; I had made sure there was extra money; I had made sure there were baby-sitters available because I knew he wouldn't think of that need until the last minute. I thought of everything and then I waited. Then, as usual, I lost out!"

Such incidents spawn rage at men. It seems men keep women from fulfilling their dreams. It becomes painfully clear that it is futile to wait for men to know how to love right; but, if they do not wait for this longed-for connection with men, where will they find the kind of satisfaction that is missing in their lives?

Julie heard a speaker at a workshop once comment that men are a lot of work and impossible to understand! Everyone had laughed. Then the speaker went on to add that the anger women house is complex, mixing as it can with three separate but related awakenings: a) the awareness of how long they have fruitlessly waited for special love; b) the awareness that their hope is placed in men's ability to change rather than in their own growth; and c) the acknowledgment of the tendency for women to feel responsible for the life of the relationship.

These potentially useful insights can initially sabotage women's relationships with men because the insights spark long held disappointment toward men. Yes, women are responsible for distorted thinking and for being over-functional but they know also that men have contributed to the difficulties in these three areas, too. So rage spurts out in globs and mixes with fear, loss of direction, and exhaustion.

Women feel betrayed by men and often, it is angry energy that catapults them out of the waiting room. Julie does not want to give up on Tom again, but she cannot figure out how to take care of herself better without also distancing from him. She still feels abandoned, backed by many memories of family needs and activities Tom missed for one reason or another.

Women have been disillusioned by men before. However, women did not have power to do anything about it. Many women went to their graves sad and lonely, but loyal and generous to a fault. Now, women have options, always with a price. Julie knows this very well. She is scared because her marriage hangs in the balance. At least she and Tom are trying to move beyond their illusions about each other. Denial was a lonely place, fraught with pain, and burdened by hard, unsatisfying work; but it created something to do: Wait and sacrifice, sacrifice and wait!

When women make "waiting" sacred, they create a dilemma for themselves with men. Men simply do not understand and therefore cannot validate the woman's "thing" with sacrifice and waiting. When the waiting room mentality is not acknowledged by women, they lump all men together in one distasteful pot. This pot thickens and boils when they share their stories with each other!

51

Still counting minutes between contractions, Julie retraces her own steps in loving Tom. "I've done a better job than Tom in caring for our marriage. I understand intimacy better than Tom. I tried for years to teach him how to be intimate, with varying degrees of success." Julie now knows that, by taking the teacher position, she took responsibility for the success or failure of their marriage. Even now, as quick as she is to blame Tom for his wrongdoings and indiscretions, she feels responsible for the outcome of this marriage, as if there must be something more she should do to make them work as a couple.

"What did Maggie once tell me about men?" The words come back to Julie as Maggie's distress increases. "Julie, there are some facts you need to understand about men. First, men have different ways of loving. Give them some slack. Second, with so much anger sizzling inside, you miss what men, and your man in particular, do offer! Third, my dear sister, you have to let Tom find his own place in the marriage; his needs in marriage are different than yours. Tom may need more time to articulate his, but that is no reason for you to help him out." Ouch! No mincing of words here!

Maggie wasn't finished. "Fourth," she had said, "you must stop waiting for Tom to satisfy that special love-feeling. Waiting already makes you angry. Letting go of waiting will stir up more anger for a while. But it is the only way to go. When I realized my husband wasn't intending to hurt me, even though it felt like it, our problems seemed more workable. If you continue to wait magically for Tom to validate your waiting and self-sacrifice, you will stay angry and unhappy in this marriage, despite your hard work and many accomplishments. Divorce will be the only answer for you both."

Julie ponders these things during a scurry of activity. It is time to bring forth a son. Maggie is ready; the child's head is pushing through. Julie closes her thoughts: "Tom and other men have been on a separate journey, coming from different roots. Maybe all my best intentions and hard work are not the keys to a successful marriage."

Julie sighs deeply, then smiles at her sister and the newborn child, while tears stream down her face. Her new nephew is beautiful.

An hour or so later, while mother and baby become acquainted, Julie drives home, not understanding why tears again fill her eyes. She speaks aloud all the way home.

I *am* capable of intimacy . . . with my children, my girlfriends and even with myself. I know what I want with Tom, but I can no longer try to teach him how to satisfy my intimacy needs. Maybe I have to throw my map over the edge and start over. But there's a lot Tom doesn't do well in our marriage. I cannot excuse all his self-interests, complacency and forgetfulness. If I do not tend to the relationship, who will? I really don't want the task; it fell into my lap. What will happen now? Who *will* remember to call his folks or remember that one of the kids has a play at school? It's hard to let go. Yet, maybe waiting for him to change isn't the answer either. I am confused.

I feel so alone; why am I all of a sudden so raw? My fear cannot be from aloneness. What will be left if I give up my understanding of marriage? I feel defeated, cheated. But what did I do so wrong? I only loved Tom with my heart and soul. I didn't try to hurt him; I didn't cheat on him. I endured a lot in the name of loving him. If I did not love him the right way, then I am at a loss on how to love him or anyone else. How does one love? Such a mystery! Does Tom need me for anything? And if he does not need me, will he still love me?

I am frightened. If Tom doesn't love me, then I feel like a failure.The fear is growing, but so is the truth. I have come too far to turn back now. How weary I am waiting for him anyway! It's hard, lonely, angering work! I have believed Tom's becoming more connected to the family is the answer to my life's needs. Even though I have a great job at the library and am well respected, I am not happy. I have to turn away from him now and hope he eventually finds his way to my heart. It is very hard to turn away my gaze.

I am not angry this time. I am scared and a little defeated but solid and firm in who I am. I see it now. *My* idea of how he should love me will block him from coming to me *his* way. I have never wanted to teach him. I have only wanted him to choose me all the way. For Tom to love me, I must get out of his way and see what happens. Truth tells me he is not very far away. Maybe he already chooses me and I cannot see it yet.

Funny how I feel inside. I am hopeful and a little excited. I even feel relieved. I have nothing to lose now and everything to gain. "Tom, can you hear me? I am not going to wait for you anymore. I am going to take better care of myself. I've been blinded by you. I've waited for you to give my life meaning. You can't do it! I'm sorry that I put that task on you. I have to find meaning and purpose separate from you. Will you still love me? Will you still want to be married to me? Will you take more notice of family needs ? I hope so. But the waiting is finally over. I cannot focus on you anymore at my own expense. I do not have much to give you right now."

Dear God, I place my hope in you. Show me how to live. Tell me what to do next. I truly do not know where to begin.

CHAPTER 6
ALONE TOGETHER

It is indeed ironic that togetherness for couples in trouble begins anew by entering a state of aloneness that propels them out of despair into a strangely empowering peace. Painful truth surrounds them. The man surveys his wreckage alone and the woman leaves the waiting room also alone. Both have exposed their personal truths, becoming free for the first time since they fell in love. Both again share a similar experience. The couple is in sync while not feeling in love. Their respective anguish may indeed not be obvious to the other.

Failure encircles them. Having compromised much of their uniqueness for love, they are horribly disillusioned; this time, in themselves. They now realize they lost themselves trying to stay together.

Here is the possibility of a new beginning! If the man and woman glance over, they can see each other again . . . masks off, defenses down, despair hanging out, and spent, no bullets to dodge or jibes to return. They have no more answers and very few questions.

Most couples call it quits right here because they simply do not know what else to do. They do not look up. If by chance they do look at the partner, they usually see the anger they expect to see but not the pain. Therefore, they do not see the true other. Since they only see some outer manifestations of pain, like anger, they conclude the relationship must go.

Dare to look hard and go beyond the anger. See your partner's pain. It is there to be seen. Like finding shells on the sandy ocean floor while snorkeling, one has to know how to discern the half-hidden treasures. At first glance, all one sees is sand. Look again and see your partner's pain. It does not look the way you look when you are in pain. But then it never did. That was part of the problem. He/she is different from you. Now, see the pain. Then, do not do anything! Sit still! Sit with the pain of aloneness—together. Do

55

not talk; do not touch; do not joke. Be together—not trying to change your mate, not trying to change yourself. Sit quietly with the mutually experienced loss and despair—the shared negative feelings. This is the first new mutuality.

Some of you reading this page may be skeptical about the potential of shared pain to restore love. In some instances, you may be right. Couples who have held in their pain for fifteen or twenty years often burst out of marriage when the pain is exposed, never to return. They do not even look back, let alone dare to sit with the other, alone together. Some people say they feel dead inside or that they have callouses on their hearts. These folks may indeed have also waited too long. Some men and women are married to people who are not able to partner with them and probably never will. For these people, there may be no standing alone together.

Men and women who are able to tolerate their own pain enough to see the pain in their partners can now experience the mutuality of an experienced aloneness. Do not pass over this thought lightly. This mutuality represents the foundation of a new intimacy in which neither partner tries to meet the expectations of the other nor demands anything in return. This is crucial because *they have finally put down their measuring sticks for determining the degree of the other's love.*

It no longer matters whether or not the other responds to the love as offered. What matters in this decisive moment is *how* they plan to do what they are going to do next. The question is not so much whether to divorce or stay together as it is *whether or not they will regard the partner in the decision.* There is a choice to be made here. How one makes it depends on what lies in the heart of one's soul. In taking the next step, there is an equal opportunity to destroy the other or allow them life. Everyone must choose alone and take responsibility for this choice. It has nothing to do with who the partner is, what they did, or what they never did for you. It has to do with you, alone!

All men and women make the choice to value or destroy a loved one over and again when they feel violated in

56

significant relationships, whether or not they acknowledge it. Distortions of each other's private idiosyncrasies can be paraded in public to soothe a wounded ego. "He was cruel to the kids." "She was a lousy sex partner." "He lied to me for years." "She never made a decision without talking to her mother!" No one forces another to hold another life sacred or destroy it. That orientation is written in one's moral code. All men and women are accountable for this choice. The degree to which they do not take ownership of their responses determines the degree to which they fall prey to evil temptations to destroy the other in the name of self-preservation.

Again, we are not addressing whether Tom and Julie divorce or stay together. We are concerned with how they act toward the other in the decision making process. Tom and Julie, alone together, must now choose independently whether they will *honor* the other in this decision. This becomes the first decision! They look at each other with eyes that see more than yesterday and talk a little.

Tom tells Julie how difficult it has been for him every time he reached out for her and she turned away. In his reality, she left him years ago when their first child was born. He reveals how much during the last year he has been trying to tune into family matters and has not shut down as much as before. Tom confesses he distanced when Julie had an emotional crisis because he did not know what to do. He does not know how she sees him today, but inside he *knows* he is more present. Mostly, he wants her to know that for a long time he was not sure he wanted to be married to her, that he was very concerned about their sex life, and that he thought he might have to end the marriage because what they shared was empty and very painful. He wants her to know that he cannot handle much more pain and he does not know how long he can endure the loneliness even now.

Initially hesitant and edgy, Tom glances briefly towards Julie who holds her gaze on him while he speaks. Sadness guides their visual exchange.

Tom's honesty challenges Julie to share some of her new insights. Funny, if Tom had told her yesterday all that he just shared, she would have jumped for joy because he was finally telling her how he felt and what he needed. Not today. Now she must tell him that he is no longer her first priority. She is uncertain about her feelings for him. She knows she loves him; she does not want to divorce him; but she is afraid that getting too close to him right now might break the connections she's recently made with herself. She has been given a gift of retrieving her life and she cannot relinquish that in the name of marriage ever again. Can she integrate her legitimate self-interests and still be married to Tom? She's a free spirit now longing for a playmate, and Tom's not wearing the right play clothes.

Julie bites her tongue, not wanting to be harsh or hurtful. But compromises are no longer an option. She wants to tell Tom why she's not happy. She studies his face and drinks in his anguish. It surprises her and touches her in the same breath. Then Julie opens up to Tom. She tells him that she cannot give him right now the love he requests but she can tell him her truths. Julie shares her need to develop herself separately from him. She stops herself from embracing him.

Oddly, Julie feels close to Tom now, respect pushing through mountains of bitterness. Tom, also, is alone with an unfamiliar tenderness surfacing towards Julie. They do not want to be married, and they do not want to be divorced. They do not know exactly what they want anymore.

Tom and Julie are sharing the intimacy of their true selves in their great disappointment. Outside the fog of anger and hurt, they can see each other. Perhaps they should say, "Hello! There you are. I was wondering where you were."

Suddenly, they are not alone. The realization is transforming! They share the same reality, feelings, predicament, and distress, but they are not alone! They are alone, together. There is a great difference between being alone and being alone together. A little hope can now enter. It will be short-lived, but it has shown its honest face and will return.

Julie and Tom get a cup of coffee and sit at the table.

In the quiet moment they assess each other and reflect on what they have said and what they have heard. Now they must rest on their own truths. They have both changed. Tom, following through on a goal to connect more to the emotional aspects of his family, has come a long way, even though it is not enough for Julie. Regardless of what Julie thinks, he is learning to validate himself separate from her approval. Julie has struggled to know herself better and be more satisfied with her choices in life even though Tom does not participate in them.

Tom and Julie look at each other long and hard. Alone together at this juncture and free from the distractions of anger and blame, Tom and Julie begin to see each other. Being separated, they now find unity. The ability to see now allows them to hear, and it comes home to them in a new way that they are different people, with different needs, and perhaps have really been on different journeys. If so, they could not have been each other's solution no matter how they tried. Perhaps, they did not fail each other after all!

This couple only glimpses these truths at this time. Nothing has congealed, but something hopeful excites and entices them. They are in delicate places, more fragile than either realizes, and endangered by the power of their cravings for the old love-feeling basis for marriage. Because they feel tender towards each other right now, they are vulnerable to being seduced by love-feelings again. It would be easy to pretend that if they now tried a little harder, love-feelings would blossom fully and save this relationship (and they would not have to go any further into this thing called aloneness). But if they pursue these love-feelings at this point, it will only be a matter of time before they will fall into the familiar trap of demanding to be loved on their own terms. They will lose sight of the other person—again! However, even if this happens (as it does to so many couples), they will quickly return to the inevitable aloneness through the door of feeling lonely and deprived, only this time with more despair and greater loss. The chase will never end until they concede the impossibility of receiving love on their own terms. They will either stand alone now in this moment of truth and make the choice to let go of their dream marriage or they will do so at another date in the future. Mature love cannot grow in love-feeling soil. Mature love comes from shared aloneness.

This truth is elusive. What *feels* like failure in love (the loss of love-feelings) for them both is really growth toward mature love. The seduction is to believe the love-feelings are love. This is an illusion! They need to remain with the sense of failure, the depression, the pain, the longing, and whatever else burdens their hearts for a little while longer and see where it brings them. This is the momentous decision time we mentioned earlier in this chapter. It is time to:

a) see love-feelings as a seductive trap;
b) sit still without knowing what will happen next; and
c) decide not to destroy the other, no matter what!

These decisions will not be made from cognitive places alone. They are not intellectual and dispassionate, nor derived from feelings. They are made by believing in something bigger than either partner alone, by having faith in a process. It is intuited more than known at this point.

Very few couples choose to remain still when they reach the threshold on which Tom and Julie stand. It tests everyone's strength and tolerance level; it demands they search their souls. To remain in each other's presence with this amount of pain leaves each partner quite vulnerable to the other. It is as if they are stripped naked and risk additional injury when not the slightest bit of negativity can be endured. Death lurks around the corner—no one wants to move. Like an unexpected noise at the base of a mountain of snow, one sound could trigger the avalanche.

Tom and Julie have reached the threshold of intimacy. They see very little of each other during the next week, pondering deeply their needs and expectations of marriage in the light of their new realizations.

CHAPTER 7
THE INTIMACY THRESHOLD

Tom and Julie are alone together on the threshold of new life. Clearly, they do not realize this fact. For them, the world has gone up in smoke. They are precariously balanced on the edge of painfully familiar scripts. The slightest breeze could cause a premature break. In truth, any quick movement could damage or break down what is forming in and between them. The silence in the air screams with energy as their minds race with contradicting thoughts.

> Julie: "If I open to him again, I risk being very hurt. I am far enough away now to bypass the tug of the love that still lingers for him. But he's saying words I've wanted to hear for a long time. Maybe this experience is changing him, too. Maybe, just maybe, we could love each other in a new way. Still, I have hoped before in vain . . . "

> Tom: "She's been so cold towards me. Nothing I do seems to penetrate that icicle. I should let her go. I have been so devastated by her rejection of me, I could not be hurt anymore, especially if I stay away. Sure, I'll let this anger keep me away. But damn it all! I do not want her to go. I know there is good love under the rubble. Should I set aside this anger? God, I want her back in my arms. But I cannot stand here like a fool much longer and let her beat me up with her eyes. Something has to happen soon. I do not know what to do next."

The couple does not know what to do on this threshold. Neither can stay very long, sensing the next step might drop them off a cliff into an abyss. In truth, it opens a new universe. No matter when they decide, the step will be risky, taken on faith, and with no guarantees of firm footing ahead.

THE LEAP OF FAITH

There is a wonderful scene in a *Star Trek, The Next Generation* episode in which one of the female characters stands on the edge of an open spaceship port gazing into space. The blackness of night before her is offset only by the sparkle of the stars.

In the story, the woman is told this space is merely an allusion—it is not empty space at all. She is also told in order to save her life and the vessel, she must go to another part of the ship through this door and only this door. To get where she needs to go, she must step out into this apparent space; it is the logical conclusion given all the data. Yet, every fiber of her being believes the space will envelop her and she will die. The story line dictates she will die anyway if she does not go to the other place on the ship.

The woman holds her breath and slowly takes the step into deep space. Her back foot must actually leave the floor inside the doorway before the front foot lands on another part of the ship. She must take this leap of faith to reach her actual destination. The decision to leap is guided by several factors: imminent danger, no way back, and her belief that it is the right thing to do.

The leap takes her across a threshold. Stepping onto firm ground, there is much relief and some new fear in addition to new hope. Something has happened outside her frame of reference she did not expect. By God, it worked! Maybe there is more ahead.

Tom and Julie are contemplating their leap of a lifetime. Maybe there is more ahead for them also. They cannot see the step. Nothing in their current history with each other advises them to take this step together. Still in anguish and fear, they wait a little longer.

A THRESHOLD

The word *threshold* brings several images to mind. First and most obvious is the doorway over which a groom carries his bride, signifying the new life they are to enter together. A second use of the word refers to the amount of pain one endures before one screams; people are said to have a high or a low threshold of pain. A third connotation suggests a brink, an edge; someone may be on the threshold of making an important discovery. All three cases apply to our developing story.

A threshold can be a stopping point, where one searches for the next step. One might decide what to do when one reaches that point. One may be intrigued and challenged to go further despite the fear which marks the edge of the known and the unknown, the perceived security of the familiar and the dreaded perils of the roads never traveled. One may become terrified and turn back, maybe even closing off in one's mind the memory of ever having been there. Fear can be a powerful motivator or deterrent.

THE ROLE OF FEAR

When discussing intimacy and its threshold, fear must be addressed. Many people reach thresholds of new opportunity and do not cross into them due to fear. They reach the end of the road on which they have been traveling and do not know what to do. They cannot comprehend the possibility of a new experience. They desperately want the old way to work, the old road to take them someplace new.

Those who divorce a mate who is depressed, severely addicted to a chemical substance, or rageful and violent, and then miraculously find new partners who are exactly the same fall into this category. They are in denial about the uselessness of the old road upon which they travel. Eventually, after coming to the same old place, they realize the truth about the limitations of their relationships. They know their lives are in shambles, but the fear of choosing a new, unknown path paralyzes them.

Because each is afraid to change the course of their own lives, blaming the other for failures is easy. Even though all the attempts to lead the other to change his/her ways lead to frustration and stagnation, they conclude it is safer to prod the other into change than to face their fears and

step out into a new direction. Fear keeps them trying old
solutions that never work. These statements are common:

* "If only he/she would stop flirting,
we might have a chance at making
this relationship work."

* "If only he/she would go to counseling, our lives would change for the
better."

* "I am devastated by what my partner
did yesterday, but if I do not talk
about it, the pain will go away and
everything will be okay again."

* "I am sure my partner is having an
affair; so I will become more desir-
able to him/her and it will end."

* "I am lonely and unhappy, and I do
not know what is the matter; I will get
busy at work (at sports, or children's
activities, or drink) and think about it
tomorrow."

THE INTIMACY OF TRUTH

The above quotes reflect people's fear of facing the
truth about their lives. Fear cripples people—fear of feeling
pain or anger, fear of risking the end of a relationship by
confronting unacceptable behavior, or fear of revealing discontent and loneliness in a marriage.

Coming to terms with the truth about themselves and
the truth as they know it about their partners crosses them
into intimacy . . . not the intimacy of love-feelings, but the
intimacy of Truth. When the love a couple shares is not
grounded in truth, there cannot be intimacy. The truth
referred to here forces people to address sensitive issues like

the ones mentioned above. Statements like these replace the old ones:

* "Your flirtatious behavior causes me a great deal of pain. I will have to stop going places with you."

* "I'm sorry you do not see counseling as a way to address our problems. I will just have to go myself and hope this will not divide us more."

* "I am going to tell _____ how much he/she hurt me even if this means he/she will be mad."

* "I will confront _____ about my strong feeling that he/she is having an affair. I will not accept his/her denial when I know in the pit of my stomach it is true. I am no longer having sex until this feeling goes away."

* "I am so unhappy I am going to sit down in this chair until something inside myself changes."

Truth also involves being able to take care of oneself without devaluing one's partner. We are talking about every man and woman's inner truth, which does not involve the other. Adults are alone with their truths. The partner need not share that truth. However, if men and women cannot overcome their fear of the consequences of speaking their own truth and escape the prison of denial, they can never reach the levels of intimacy they desire.

The troubles and conflicts which haunt couples today compel them to come to terms with their own Truth—needs, hopes, dislikes, fears, and all. If they do not come to terms with these issues now, they will only be forced to face this same truth again in the future around a different issue with the same or a different partner.

The truth talked about here is a personal truth about intuitions, needs, and perspectives on reality. One's truth may not be shared by the partner nor even be validated by the other. Nothing the other can say will change this truth anyway. Truth is the only real path upon which one can take the next step. Stating this truth out loud, no matter what it is or how it is received, is the only requirement for stepping off the threshold.

Personal truth is the keystone of intimacy. It is the only quality strong enough to sustain the self in the face of emotional disintegration, and it is the only quality clear enough to define the problems. *If men and women have nothing but availability to their own truths, they have what it takes to realize intimacy.* They have their integrity and no one can take that away from them. With personal honesty they have something to hold onto, they have something to offer another, and they are free to receive another without fear of being blown away. The belief in one's own truth protects the self from perceived annihilation. This level of truth sharing characterized Julie and Tom's last encounter.

The intimacy of truth demands that couples let go of the armor of fear, denial, and self-protection. In so doing, they stand naked before one another in a most vulnerable state. Couples who present themselves at this altar of emotional nakedness are ready to step off the threshold. They have all they need; this is the logical conclusion!

Julie and Tom have done that much. They have told themselves and each other the truth. Julie let Tom know how very dissatisfied she had been with him as a partner for a long time. Tom told Julie how shut out he felt and that he too was questioning his place in the marriage. They now stand naked and needy before each other. They may not accept each other's truth. That is not the primary concern at this moment. They are intimately bonded through *their own truth* and whatever they choose next can and will bear fruit. There are prices to be paid for moving forward. Tom and

Julie, and all couples in their situation, need to redress at this point their original contracts for marriage and cut away that which is not compatible with their present truths. The stripping away process which has led them to the threshold has strengthened them, even though they do not really believe this yet. They now have the ability to pay the price for intimacy because their personal truths make it affordable.

Some early catalysts for marrying are no longer compatible with healthy union. These truths must be addressed on the threshold as well. For example, a woman might realize, "I married you because we had sex, not because I really wanted to be with you," or "I married you to get out of my home." A man may reflect, "I married you because I thought no one else would have me," or "I married you so no one else could have you."

Confronting fear of the unknown and coming to terms with the truth are the two major prerequisites of stepping over the threshold of intimacy. Couples must also abandon old baggage to travel in the new space. The delicate journey necessitates that one travel lightly only with courage, faith, and truth. The following articles of old baggage must be left behind at the threshold of intimacy.

LOVE-MAPS

Individual love-maps must go! They have limited and confined love to idiosyncratic designs long enough. Now, fraught with self-righteousness, stereotypes, and prejudice, old love-maps blind couples and compound the growing sense of isolation. Stereotypes especially reinforce the sense of alienation and the fear of a mismatched marriage, confusing the couple into thinking they should find someone more like them than their present partner.

Each must now develop the capacity to learn and appreciate the other's unique language of love. In honoring their own truths, they will not have to surrender their own language, only be willing to learn at least the rudimentary elements of the other's. They need not become expert linguists, only be able to translate accurately. The couple can stand together, even if their love languages are worlds apart.

THE INDISPENSABLE

There is usually one ingredient in marriage which every man and woman can single out as most vital and significant to sustain their relationship. It probably is not the same item for any two people because all men and women have different ways of recognizing they are valued. Each pursues with dogged determination the realization of that one element of love in a package tailored for them. This component seems to be indispensable in a fulfilling marriage.

What is usually felt as indispensable is a demand from a fearful part of oneself to be loved a certain way to repair lingering unhealed wounds from an earlier time. If not acknowledged as such, the desired ingredient can only become a desperate demand on the partner.

"If you really loved me, you would . . . would not . . . etc."; "If you really loved me, I would not have to . . ." Such demands do not a marriage make. Marriage is a union, in which the responsibility for correcting a problem lies chiefly with one's self, not the other.

When Sally and Joe married, for example, the families celebrated the union. Sally and her mother were very close, and Sally turned to her father for a lot of decisions. Joe, married previously, was close to his seven- and ten-year-old sons who lived with their mother but kept a comfortable distance from his own parents. Sally non-verbally demanded that Joe defer to her family like she did and not upset them. Joe demanded, in like manner, that Sally treat his children as though they were her own and defer to their needs upon demand. Joe felt hurt when Sally turned to her family for all decisions as though he did not count; Sally felt hurt when Joe changed their plans for an evening or weekend because the boys needed something. Each wanted to be received by the other with their own baggage but not the other's! If this couple cannot give up what seems indispensable, the relationship will wither.

Jill and Karl planned a vacation together. They had been working very hard establishing a new business and had not taken a "real" vacation in two years. They really needed one! Jill disliked skiing but loved touring. She wanted to go to Europe. Karl really disliked traveling and could feel how great skiing down his favorite western slopes would be. Having grown up in families where their own choices were not valued enough, they fought ferociously over this impasse. The vacation was canceled, and they blamed each other. What they needed to surrender was a rigid picture of how the vacation should look . . . not the vacation itself. Because they each had an indispensable contingency on the plans, negotiations for mutual satisfaction could not advance.

The demands to satisfy "the indispensable" transfer love into anger which inevitably leaks into the marriage. Men and women cannot remain angry about unfulfilled needs and expect intimacy to evolve. They also cannot postpone their own needs in service of the other's needs, secretly waiting for the mate to do the same in return and expect not to become angry. This will only lead to more frustration and distance. Both skiing and touring must not become indispensable for a vacation to take place.

ROMANCE

There is this notion that all lovemaking should be exciting, romantic, fresh, and new with every encounter. For most couples, that myth sells books and movies only. Average couples experience a range of attraction to each other that varies quite a bit. It goes with the territory. To demand that love be "felt" as special every day puts a tremendous burden on the marriage.

Larry likes sex . . . a lot! He could enjoy sex two or three times a day if his partner were available and interested. Getting ready for sex is a big part of Larry's sense of romance. Beth likes sex, too . . . a lot! But a lot for her is once or twice a week. He wants her to be enticing every day; she wants him to court her and seduce her once a week. For Beth, romance is felt in quiet talks over dinner, walking hand in hand on the beach, and knowing Larry really loves her. Neither of them will receive, on a sustained basis, the kind of romance which lives in their heads. If couples link their love with their idiosyncratic "feelings" of romance, they will conclude love is waning.

The kind of romance Larry and Beth think they want is rooted in uncertainty, in wondering if the other chooses and desires them or not. Their love is only exciting, makes their hearts skip beats, makes them sweaty, and helps them become lost in the swirl of emotional upsurge only when the relationship is uncertain. This kind of romance dissipates when uncertainty is replaced by the couple's choosing each other as covenant partners. Now that they have ritually consummated their love, uncertainty disappears and so may romance. The fascination with romance must be left behind if intimacy is to be realized. Loss of romance on this plane is the price of committed monogamy.

SEXUAL FULFILLMENT

Sex is not always satisfying within a monogamous relationship. Partners do not always satisfy each other. No one has failed or is necessarily disinterested. It is merely a fact of life. To choose to cross the threshold into intimacy, couples must surrender an exciting sex life as the fulfilling goal. This demand on marriage is also too burdensome, calling forth blame and hurt and leading to threats of unfaithfulness.

Sex outside of marriage is exciting because of the allure of an unknown other. The newness of the body and/or the personality provides the excitement. However, within marriage, the partners are getting to know each other well. Therefore, sexual excitement must necessarily wane. An exciting sexual life cannot sustain a relationship alone. One must continually find new tricks to heighten the excitement in much the same way as more of a drug is needed to sustain a high. We build up a tolerance for sexual excitement. This is why a demand for exciting sex must also go.

"ONENESS"

The expression "we are one" is misleading! Couples are not and never will be of one mind on a great percentage of the issues they must resolve together. Even when they are of one mind on what should be done, they often differ on how they should proceed. The words a woman uses will differ greatly from the words a man will use to encourage someone's participation with them on a project. Couples are not one. They are two minds, two hearts, two very different languages, and two separate beings. They cannot possibly build intimacy on "oneness;" however, they ought not pursue divorce on the awareness of their differences.

When couples fall in love, mutuality abounds! They seem to be linked together in every possible way. One could have a thought the other finishes; one shows up at the front door while the other is placing a call. They dream the same dream in the same words and know exactly what the other is thinking. The swoon from the heightened energy electrifies the air. It is awesome. They cannot keep their eyes off each other, let alone their hands. They must call each other after spending a twelve hour day together. They agree easily to every movie, meal, and mad activity; a wonderful stage for them but most difficult for family members who cannot wait for this stage to end.

When couples marry, they unfortunately expect this oneness to continue and experience a let-down when it ends. They often place the burden of oneness back on their relationship as a test of love. Love means they agree; non-love is represented by disagreement. Oneness is not the norm! To demand this unrealistic unity forces a polarized situation of "I'm right; you're wrong!"

CONSENSUAL REALITY

A great deal of maturity is required to stand alone with one's definition of reality, of the truth, if you will, while a partner disclaims it right and left. One couple tried to tell mutual friends about a visit from the wife's mother. The husband said the problems centered around the mother's lack of mobility. If she had a car, she would have enjoyed herself better. The wife said transportation was not a problem at all. The problem was around his not being available to the family for planned outings. This couple spent the better part of an hour trying to convince each other in front of a court of their friends who was right and therefore who must be wrong. They could not agree, no matter how much they tried to overpower and outwit each other. This kind of activity between spouses is a complete waste of energy and causes a lot of destruction. They will never convince the partner of their own version of reality. This must be relinquished; it is a dead end. They do not need consensus on reality. What they do need is a handle on their own reality and an ability to articulate it to themselves so they can later ask for what they need from the other. They can let the other frame the entire problem differently if the other must. One's own truth does not violate anyone else's truth but merely stands alongside the other reality.

If consensual reality remains a prerequisite for love, all problems or differences are threatening. Insisting on consensual reality in marriage denies differences which otherwise might bring life and spice to the union. But more importantly it also denies the right of the other to exist. This is too high a price to pay to be in a relationship. Consensual reality is too costly and must go.

SELF-RIGHTEOUSNESS AND
THE HIGHER MORAL GROUND

An atmosphere that demands oneness and consensual reality cannot house two equal but different participants. One or the other always jumps into the driver's seat. One or the other becomes eloquent on a subject, takes an authoritative stand and thereby intimidates the other. Competition, defensiveness, and a spirit of breaking down the other become tools of accomplishing one's task to have oneness his or her way.

Claiming higher moral ground always implies the devaluation of the other. Like sitting on a teeter-totter, when one is up, the other is down. Couples in conflict always bring themselves up with their strengths and put the other down for their frailties. In many marriages men become the eloquent experts on some subjects and women on the others. They create some pseudo-balance which satisfies for a while but lacks sustaining power. Even though each can be an expert on some things, each is also devalued on others. Intimacy cannot survive devaluation. Self-righteousness must go!

CONTROL

Control must be forfeited because it negates the co-authorship of the relationship. In an equal, intimate relationship no one is in control. To be in control automatically subordinates the other and thereby compromises intimacy. If either partner uses control of the other to abate anxiety , the relationship will die. One cannot enjoy the benefits of equality without surrendering control. One can, however, have influence!

THE DREAM

All men and women have a particular dream about marriage. For only a short while they seem to share the same dream. The powerful pull of a shared dream forms a wave that lifts a couple high up onto a given set of values which cannot be sustained as normal differences emerge or change due to natural evolution. The dreams, embedded as they are in what seem to be culturally and familiarly projected values, all have happy endings; no one is hurt or abandoned; everyone's needs are eventually met through love.

Many people dream of being a perfect family. They conjure up images that would satisfy the dream, fulfill their life's work, redeem them in some fashion for life's past disappointments. They plan the results of life before they take all the real steps along the road. The dream at first sustains them through hope; then later, it fuels anger towards the mate who becomes the reason for the loss of the dream.

Dreams on this plane reflect one's own relationship to a family of origin, either in the attempt to duplicate it or in trying to create the opposite. Couples unwittingly fight with each other over whose family of origin's ways will prevail in their own home. One woman came from a family in which the mother made all the important decisions; her husband came from a family in which the father had been the dominant figure. They were most confused when the other could not respect their authority. This couple also struggled with numerous family traditions. What seemed right for one contradicted a valued part of history for the other. Holidays, birthdays, and ways of showing love all come into question when dealing with couples' dreams. Dreams on this plane must also be left behind.

INTERPRETATIONS

Joe suggested an alternative plan to a friend with whom he had an upcoming scheduled activity. Ten men and women were to meet at Joe's home to bring in the new year. He suggested a place to go dancing if that might be more appealing to the group. After he asked a friend to relay the question to one of the guests, word came back to him that several people declined his invitation because they thought he wanted to go dancing. They really had no interest in that activity. To be nice and give him lots of room to change plans, they said they were tired anyway, were going out to dinner early and really wanted to stay home. This was, of course, never Joe's intention. When he questioned his friend on how she presented the dancing opportunity, she said she had spoken for him and probably should not have done so. She said she told them he was tired, very busy, and it would be much easier on him if he did not have to prepare his home for a party!

This double interpretation, which missed Joe's intentions altogether, is a small example of the dilemmas couples face when they think they know what each other wants or thinks or needs. Couples need to surrender a belief that they can accurately interpret each other's actions, words, and intentions for themselves or to the community-at-large. Private interpretation is a dangerous activity which elevates one's own version of reality over the other without the benefit of a possible rebuttal.

Here's another example: Jill waited an hour for Scott in the parking lot. When he finally arrived, he was mad at Jill for not running the errands she had agreed to earlier. He immediately interpreted this behavior as her fear of driving in rush hour traffic. Jill responded that he was wrong, but

Scott heard nothing because he "knew Jill better than she knew herself."

Interpretation and all the other detractors to good relationships mentioned above are not conducive to intimacy because they superimpose one of the partners over the other. There is inequality between them. One's reality, dream, interpretation, and love fantasy are unique, personal, and preclude the other.

SUMMARY

At the threshold of intimacy neither partner demands his or her reality. It simply does not matter anymore. Each is convinced that nothing can change the other or the situation. Separateness has been reached and private demands have died in the process. This is necessary for intimacy to emerge.

The problems with establishing mutuality are clearly enormous. Paradoxically, the more couples receive each other in true separateness, the less trouble they will find. If couples can leave behind popular cultural prescriptions for sustaining relationships and stick to the truth, intimacy can emerge unencumbered.

Intimacy begins in the "stripping away of the ideals" process. When men or women admit they cannot have exactly what they want and think they need from the other, they must accept what is there. Intimacy can only emerge when people take the risk to give up what they think is essential in love for them to experience intimacy. All that is really necessary is the true self and the true other.

The intimacy threshold is a real but intangible place; it is the edge of the old and the doorway to the new. Most people are terrified of it. Most people redirect their needs for the "oneness" they have not found onto a new other, rather than give up what feels like a sacred right, i.e., to have it. Some people gather others around them who sing the same song they sing. They create a formidable defense for truth, justice, and their way! They maintain their right for romance, sexual fulfillment, demanding "the indispensable," and holding onto an impossible dream. Also, mandates for consensual reality define marriage for them; so, they feel alone. The loneliness is the other's fault, of course.

Those who reach the threshold have decisions to make. The above baggage must go. The task is difficult and risky but necessary to find love built upon equality. If we were not forced by our problems to take this leap, most of us might not cross over.

Tom and Julie are not cognitively thinking about any of these things anymore. They have been using all available energy to stay present in the moment, not to run away, not to anticipate divorce, but to trust their own emerging intimacy of truth. Soon, they will each need to make a momentous decision. Having come this far, they will find the next step.

CHAPTER 8
REDECISION

THE CHOICE

Julie and Tom stand emotionally naked before each other at the threshold, stripped bare of their notions of love. Their expectations have sunk to the basement. Emptiness surrounds each of them. In this virgin space, something surprising happens. They have known sexual intimacy in their physical nakedness. Here, in this most unfamiliar place, they find spiritual intimacy in their emotional nakedness. They have become vulnerable and open with each other, regarding the other through eyes now more capable of giving and receiving truth. Honesty guides their exchanges; all is out in the open.

At this point, they face the biggest decision of their lives. Do they choose each other now? They chose each other once before in their physical nakedness, but do they choose each other now in their emotional nakedness? Do they want to step out into a new universe with each other, go it alone, or find someone else? They revisit the first time they decided to marry, but this time, with a greater awareness of self and the other.

MARRIAGE

What was this marriage? Was it a legal contract, an emotional bond, a covenant, or a commitment? These expressions are commonly applied to marriage, but what do they mean? What do couples mean when they say they are married or intend to marry? The answers are not absolute. Even when a couple says, "We are committing ourselves to each other to grow together in love," the meaning is not clear. In every society, a ritual is enacted when a couple joins together. They are symbols of a passage from one state to another. The past is celebrated before a new step into the future is taken. The function of a ritual is to highlight and bring out the sacred nature of passages and decisions.

In our culture, men and women choose each other in

marriage. How do they make this choice? What constitutes their decision? Do they, in fact, actually decide? Although the choice is free, many factors influence the decision. The desire to experience romance, legitimize sexual intercourse, bear children, extract oneself from unpleasant surroundings, share financial obligations, escape from loneliness, and feel valued all play a rather large role in the so-called "free choice."

Considering a life-long commitment is at stake, marriage is an awesome decision to make in conjunction with a relatively unknown entity, the prospective spouse. In a society where people commonly marry before the twenty-fifth birthday, there is hardly enough time to know oneself very well, let alone a potential mate! At best, decisions are educated guesses in an atmosphere of supposed freedom. Perhaps this is why other cultures do not leave such an important decision in the hands of young people.

Consider the anecdotes below. These individuals and couples have all faced serious decisions.

MALLORY AND SEAN

Mallory, 26, and Sean, 27, dated regularly for three years. They lived together for two years, split up several times, reunited each time, dating each other exclusively. After the last breakup, they decided to continue the relationship but live in their own apartments. This arrangement seemed to suit them best.

Mallory wanted Sean to offer marriage, but he never did. Actually, he seemed quite reticent. His lack of desire to marry affected Mallory's desire as well. Why should she want to marry someone who seemed so ambivalent? She needed a man to be more definite in choosing her to assuage her own misgivings. Still, after every two week separation, their desire for each other blossomed again, and they fell back into each other's waiting arms, reunited and consummated, the next cycle of doubt already fermenting under the surface.

Finally, the inevitable happened: Mallory became pregnant. Not wanting to give up the child, but also not wanting to bind Sean to her against his will, Mallory determined to keep the two issues separate. She would have the child as a single parent if need be and continue to leave open marriage to Sean. To Mallory's surprise, after his initial shock which included some harsh demands of her, Sean became really free to choose her in marriage. This truly gratified her. Sean was proud to be the father of their coming child. They married within five months and set off together.

THE COMMENTARY

Mallory and Sean were wise enough to realize their love-feelings were not strong enough to move them to marry, but having a child was. Mallory and Sean are not unique. This happens too often to be classified an "accident." Their decision to marry needed to go beyond feelings for each other and attach to some solid value, such as bringing children into the world under the best circumstances.

Their beliefs about how they could have children together moved Sean and Mallory beyond their ambivalence about marriage. While love-feelings were not substantial enough to help them choose marriage, family values were.

Mallory was at first skeptical, the turn-around being so great. She came to see that an enormous change really had occurred in Sean with the advent of a baby.

The crisis of pregnancy separated them emotionally. They both pulled way back. They stopped looking for guidance in love-feelings for a little while and took a hard look at their situation. They also took a hard look at each other. Mallory became free to bear a child alone. Now she could look at Sean and decide if she wanted to choose him on a stronger basis. As Sean looked at Mallory, he was forced to define his commitment to her, which he had not done before. They found over several weeks of discussion that they believed in family and each other's ability to fulfill a commitment to family . . . and they believed in each other's honest presence.

For this couple to need a stronger base for marriage

is not unusual, but rarely does a couple making this choice receive any credit for the way they approach marriage. More typically, the community labels them as inadequate or too weak to make the commitment unless forced.

Such a view is shortsighted and reflects the "shotgun marriage" mentality still prevalent in society. Intended to cover up an accident and pretend the marriage was capable of becoming a good one, "doing the right thing" meant honoring society's accepted form and condemning women who had babies alone, despite the large numbers choosing to do so. Mallory and Sean were not forced to marry. They made a choice. Society's reaction is demeaning for young couples trying to understand the nature of marriage in the nineties. Sadly, they too do not give themselves enough credit for what they have done.

Nevertheless, Mallory and Sean made a decision about their lives. This decision had little to do with their feelings and much more to do with what they valued in life, what they believed about each other, and what they concluded would be a viable and reasonable choice in response to their life situation.

These are the same bases upon which Tom and Julie and other troubled couples like them must make choices—emotionally separated from each other, tuned in to their own different needs and values, and able to think things through. They have experienced it all by now. Their feelings for each other are long past being relevant. They have been in love and out of love. They have hated each other, made up a hundred times, treated each other poorly, and have compromised themselves due to guilt feelings far too often, none of which resolved their difficulty.

Tom and Julie stand on the threshold not knowing what to do next, but alert to the need for a decision. On what will this decision be made if not upon their feelings for each other?

A familiar cliche suggests that the "darkest hour is just before the dawn." This is especially true for couples in crisis. Through the gradual breakdown of their relationship, Tom and Julie are forced to decide their fates. Does it all

80

come down to a dispassionate decision reached in the cold, hard light of day?

Tom and Julie must decide what they want. They must rechoose each other, if they can, from some new basis, like Mallory and Sean did. Although they are not having a child, Tom and Julie will have to look outside their respective feelings for help.

Below are two more examples of this redecision struggle. Take particular note of how the couples resolve their crises.

MEG AND BILL

Meg chose to marry Bill, even though he gambled a lot and frightened her. Because she believed the gambling was only due to his lack of confidence in himself and would diminish as his career evolved, she put aside her misgivings to marry anyway. She chose her role as a supportive one, determined to focus her energies on helping him in any way possible. Her unspoken codicil implicitly demanded that he become a success in his endeavors and learn to gamble in moderation.

Bill had an agenda, also. He was a frightened young man who wanted Meg to help him over his self-doubts. Meg seemed to believe she could help him; he wanted to believe that, too.

Five years later, Bill was not very successful and gambled even more. Meg was now more frightened, had three children, no income of her own, and felt trapped by her earlier decisions. She grieved to the core her prior decision to stand by him in all things. She knew now she could no longer do that. Feeling like a failure, Meg sought counsel from clergy and cried in church. The world had never seemed so dark and foreboding. But she could not live like this anymore; it was all too painful and devaluing of her. Meg knew she must leave Bill or go down with him. She could not let this happen to her or the children.

Meg's decision was now based upon self-care apart from Bill's well-being. Having spent all her energies tending to and waiting for her husband to "get it together" her way, she realized that she had to get life together for herself despite him. She felt like a traitor. Meg's decision was based upon the belief that nothing would change unless she left Bill.

As late in the game as the decision for self-care was, Meg began to feel better once the choice was made. Plans concretized, a home opened to her, and she knew the children and she would be okay. A couple of months after Meg left with the children, Bill did stop gambling and asked her to return to their home. The loss of his family became the impetus for his anguished decision to deal with his addiction. Although Meg had called his attention to it by leaving, he now knew the gambling problem was his.

Meg loved Bill. She did not really want to leave him; she only knew she could not live with him while he lied and misused their monies. With trepidation and caution, Meg and the children returned. Soon, the decision to rebuild family proved to be a good one. They had a shared purpose for the first time in their marriage. They focused on Bill's recovery process, on raising children, and on living with each other without demanding each other's life blood as part of the contract.

Meg and Bill's decisions carried them for five more years. When the children grew up and recovery no longer needed their diligent attention, the decisions which had supported them thus far gave out. The couple reached another fork in the road. In spite of their success with the family, their decisions had not drawn them together as intimate partners. They had survived a difficult time, but they still did not cherish each other. Something else had to happen for Meg or their marriage would again be in danger.

Having talked about a move out of state for eight years, the couple decided to make the break. Now, with five years' recovery, it seemed the right time. Meg planned to work in the business world as well as Bill. So, their job searches began. This plan and the ensuing activity drew them somewhat together. They again shared a goal, now to plant roots in an unknown place, buy a home, and settle down with their teenagers.

Meg's work occupied a lot of her time and energy. She loved her job and felt valued. The elements missing in her marriage were again put on the back burner because life's happenings were satisfying and rewarding. The newness and excitement carried Meg for five more years. Still, she was not united in spirit with her husband. She did not like his job choices, nor his way of doing business. To her chagrin, she did not even like him very much as a person.

Meg went into despair again, this time for three years, until a life event catapulted her to another plane. This crisis again challenged her to choose life.

Meg became sick, very sick. Bill rallied; he did not want to lose her. The physical manifestations of Meg's slipping away matched her inner withdrawal. Bill could feel this and tried to pull her back. It was too late. Meg could not choose Bill anymore as her partner. She did not die, but she did die to a marriage with Bill.

Meg closed a door and never opened to Bill again. Several particular events led to this decision. Of greatest importance was the life-cry she could no longer ignore which surfaced during her illness. Meg started testing Bill. She needed him to receive her, love her, and treat her with respect. Over and again, he evidenced an inability to do so in ways she could recognize. The marriage reached an unbridgeable impasse. She did not know what would happen, but she could not and would not live this death anymore.

After a week-long depression, Meg asked Bill for a divorce. Saying the dreaded words, Meg felt relieved . . . and then free. She felt like she had been in prison and someone just unlocked the gates to let her out. She had not loved Bill for a long time, but she had not known how to leave him. When she came back to Bill the first time, she vowed she would never leave again unless it was forever. This vow forged an endurance which almost killed her. Leaving her self-made prison, Meg began to live.

Bill was devastated by Meg's unilateral decision. His anger and hurt led him to devalue her in the community, to label her actions as evidence of her sickness or a distortion of needs. He never could understand what she wanted from him. His recovery from the loss of Meg took many years. In some ways he never did.

THE COMMENTARY

Meg's and Bill's story is both common and tragic, flawed from the very start. Meg's decision to marry Bill was based upon facilitating his life, not upon her own best interests, the core of which she had not yet come to know. She overrode her legitimate fears in favor of a role: to help the one she loved to achieve his goals. This decision was based upon the needs and well-being of another, as well as her own need to be a helper. Meg had not chosen Bill out of a healthy self-regard. She was "in love" with him, but it was not him she loved. She loved her role until she nearly drowned with him. Fortunately, Meg extracted herself before it was too late.

Bill's decision to marry was equally compromised. He did not marry Meg for companionship, he married her to shore up his nagging self-doubts. He needed someone to show confidence in him so he could feel better. Bill was no better off than Meg. He had a sense of self-interest, but an unhealthy sense. He was consumed by himself and could not see beyond his own troublesome needs.

Neither Meg nor Bill should be faulted for the basis of their decision to marry one another. They were not responsible for the emotional immaturity that characterized them in their early twenties. In doing the best they could with what they had, they followed their hearts. With nothing more substantial than love-feelings grounded in immaturity, what else could they do?

The couple's sense of love grew out of what they could complete for each other. Meg felt whole when she could care for and help someone else. Bill felt whole when someone helped him through his insecurity. In some sense, their decision to marry filled out each other's lives. Their love-feelings fed off their fantasies of where their loving would take them.

While Meg and Bill cannot be faulted for immaturity, they can be held accountable for subsequent decisions as they matured. Decisions, first made upon feelings of love, soon gave way to decisions made in spite of love.

85

LOVEWORKS

After a few years of marriage, Meg found herself forced to make decisions on the basis of a healthy self-interest and a belief in what she knew to be true. She believed Bill's gambling would destroy their family. She had to save herself, which she eventually did by leaving the first time. The situation provoked Meg out of immature love-feelings into a healthy state of self-regard and an independent assessment of her reality. In a sense, she was forced to become healthier by the situation of their marriage.

The step to leave Bill took all her strength and was not done lightly. Her life with him to this point was based upon helping him. Now she had to abandon him and help herself before it was too late. For Meg to focus on her own self-interest, let alone at the apparent expense of someone else, was unfamiliar territory. If she were not forced by Bill's secretive actions and subsequent lies, she probably would never have taken such a step. Meg stretched into a greater emotional maturity by looking after her own well-being when she felt endangered. She could not allow herself to go down with a sinking ship. With this move, Bill was also forced to a higher plane of maturity. He had to stop making excuses for himself and own up to his own problems arising from personal insecurity and addiction. He had to admit that he was preoccupied with himself and not thinking of anyone else. This was his truth and he needed to do something about it.

Both Meg and Bill had now made decisions about their lives on some basis other than love-feelings. For Meg, a healthy self-regard guided choices; for Bill, facing the truth about his insecure self gave new direction to his choices. If he wanted Meg in his life, he could no longer live preoccupied with himself. He must consider the well-being of someone else, Meg. Both had moved to a new level of maturity in this crisis and subsequently moved forward together with a fresh plan which included a relocation, an emphasis on family life, a commitment to stop gambling entirely, and new career directions for them both. This map organized and satisfied them for several years.

Now that Meg had learned to make decisions with a

self-care factor written into the equation, she faced another personal crisis. The choice of Bill as a partner in the early years came from an immature emotional need. This choice was now called into question from the higher level of maturity. The truth was beginning to dawn for Meg: She did not want to be married to Bill. She confessed to herself that she did not even like him. She did not like the way he handled himself in work, nor the way he chose to live his life. Meg put off facing this truth as long as she could until her failing health forced her out of this denial. Another decision was forthcoming, this time on the basis of the naked truth. Meg simply did not want to be with Bill, regardless of what he did or did not do. In reality, her decision had little to do with Bill. Free from her role, she could now really choose.

Meg and Bill did not really *decide* to marry. They simply went with what their hearts dictated and what was expected of them. They developed the form of a marriage but not the dynamic inner workings because the parts were not as yet manufactured.

Fortunately, marriage provokes men and women to greater maturity as their troubles unfold and escalate. In the end, people are forced to come to terms with the truth about themselves and what they really want for their lives. This is maturity.

There seems to be a natural order of events which must be regarded. One must have a healthy self before that self can combine in a healthy way with another. This is a natural evolutionary process. Meg could not make a self-interested decision about Bill until she was able to recognize her self as important and worthy to be more than only a support to someone else. Once this was established, she could look at Bill and decide if he was the person with whom she wanted to share her life.

There are basically two kinds of decisions: self-caring decisions and mutual decisions. The decision to join a relationship or remain in one must be based upon self-care interests and must come first. Then, decisions can become more mutual to honor the relationship. If the very decision to marry is not self-care based, then a person will be forced to make a self-care decision later on when the relationship is in the balance, which is what Meg had to do. Lacking self-care and self-honoring features, marriages are filled with pseudo-mutuality, the mutuality of not caring for self, which quickly runs dry.

If, however, a self-care decision is made at the beginning or later on, mutuality becomes possible. Mutual decisions are never at anyone's expense. Meg decided to extract herself from her marriage when she realized she could no longer live with the lack of mutuality. She was looking after Bill, and Bill was looking after Bill, but no one was looking after her. Not enough of Meg's self was present at the time of her marriage to override Bill's limited ability to be sensitive to her needs. To correct this problem, she made a unilateral move to reestablish herself as the grounded individual she should have become before she married Bill.

Meg did not consider standing still to let a mutual decision between herself and Bill emerge on what to do next. Meg very much needed to end her immature relationship with Bill, which she did by asking for a divorce. The request followed a heartfelt search for other viable options. None surfaced for her. Because Meg's *concept* of marriage and the *substance* of the marriage she and Bill had created were so entwined, she had to divorce Bill to end what was painfully unacceptable.

Meg boxed herself into a corner when she vowed never to leave Bill again unless it was forever. She walled off a valuable outlet. Earlier, she had moved away until Bill seemed responsive and made some changes; she returned when the relationship could move forward more mutually. This time Meg could not wait for a mutual direction to take shape. She could not treat her partner with the highest regard because years of unacknowledged pain flooded her heart. If she had, Bill, at least, would have felt regarded; not happy, but regarded.

Even at this late date, Meg and Bill could have taken a step together with the intimacy of truth expressed by Meg. Who knows what they might have done? Yes, Meg did not want to stay with Bill any longer. This is the new truth which surfaces here for her. Bill might have found that he did not want to be with her either, perhaps for different reasons. But aborting the process of intimacy by blocking discussion left Bill seeing himself as a victim of Meg and all other women like her. He would miss his own truth by focusing anger at Meg for abandoning him. Bill, for the moment, missed an opportunity to mature a little more, as well.

Let's look at another couple who dealt with their marital crisis somewhat differently.

JOHANNA AND REGGIE

Johanna and Reggie did not technically marry until some eight years into their relationship after they bore two children together. A justice of the peace married them at some point. But, as with most couples, they too had problems.

Reggie, after meeting Johanna, realized that someone really wanted him for who he was. They shared a fulfilling sexual relationship which demonstrated to him how much she valued him. After the birth of their first child, Johanna no longer desired Reggie as she once did. Although she was afraid to acknowledge this, it became very clear nevertheless. Reggie did not respond well to this new situation and put pressure on Johanna to participate in their sexual lives as she once had. This made Johanna less apt to go along with what Reggie wanted. Every argument came down to one ending: Reggie not feeling valued by Johanna and Johanna not feeling recognized by Reggie.

After five years of struggle with this issue, Reggie told Johanna that he could no longer live with her. Being in the same house with her and not having a sexual relationship was simply intolerable for him.

89

Reggie's commitment to Johanna did not include a relationship without sex. He would rather live by himself than live any longer under these conditions. He anguished over leaving his children behind, but under the circumstances, he could not stay. Reggie spent many sleepless nights in pain over the situation.

Johanna was constantly furious with what seemed like Reggie's dogged pursuit of her for sex and his apparent indifference to her needs. She wanted credit for her efforts to override her own needs to meet Reggie's. She could not recognize Reggie's responses as positive, if he was offering any. Still, Johanna did not want him to leave the home.

They knew this way of living had to end. They stood on a cliff and looked at each other. Reggie knew Johanna cared for him even though she would not participate with him sexually, and he also knew she was struggling internally. She really did want to have a good and satisfying sexual relationship with him and did not understand why she could not be more available. Even though she had some doubts about Reggie's love for her, especially in light of his seeming preoccupation with sex and wanting to move out, she knew him to be loyal, well-meaning, and devoted to his children. She did not want him to leave.

When Reggie concluded he could not tolerate the situation, he broke away from his commitment to live together. He did not, however, move out without discussing the option with Johanna. He needed Johanna to concur. Such was Reggie's way of honoring his larger commitment to the relationship, that is, to Johanna's well-being and the children's welfare. However, he would move out over her objection if nothing else more satisfactory could be worked out. He was desperate.

Johanna was distressed. Every issue between them threatened their relationship because of the sexual dilemma. The threat of Reggie's leaving hung over them like impending doom. Johanna was afraid to talk to Reggie under these conditions, but needed to do so. Talking out loud was her way of coming to a better understanding of herself. So, talk she did.

When Reggie heard Johanna's story, he offered a plan. Their youngest child would be going to school in five years. He would need at least that long to prepare their house for sale. He needed to apply himself at work during that time to earn enough money to support himself alone and help support the family household, should that be necessary. He knew he could not live the rest of his life in a sexless marriage but he could do just about anything for five years! Reggie chose to stay connected to Johanna even though he gave up on what he wanted. He agreed to honor their relationship, remaining monogamous and financially supportive.

Reggie promised to remain with Johanna in this fashion for five years; she could count on him. In exchange, he wanted Johanna to agree to a sexual relationship with him on her terms. In addition, he asked her to agree to see a therapist, either together or alone.

Johanna was scared, being so dependent on Reggie for financial support of two children. She was in much conflict over claiming the legitimacy of her own needs, still fearful of alienating Reggie more. Being in this tight spot only hindered her opening up to Reggie physically. His proposal would give her some breathing room and would relieve some pressure by guaranteeing his presence, financial support, and his continued participation in the children's lives. It also would allow both of them to delve more deeply into their issues with each other without the risk of blowing the whole relationship out the window, arbitrarily, over any one argument. This step could offer Johanna the chance to work on this situation without the threat of losing Reggie completely, at least for right now. Johanna agreed to the plan.

But Johanna was still very concerned about feeling forced to have sex with Reggie just to keep him in the home. She countered his offer suggesting he take an apartment or a room he could go to when it was too painful to be around her. At the same time, she wanted him to consider their house his home. He could come and go, stay overnight if he wanted to or go back to his own place. Johanna also indicated that freedom from pressure to meet his sexual need would probably allow her to open up more, creating greater possibilities for sex. She also agreed to therapy together. Reggie agreed to the plan. They pledged to remain monogamous for these next five years.

It would take the better part of three years to see them out of the woods. But no step was more crucial than the first step out of aloneness. Each step after that became a little easier.

THE COMMENTARY

Johanna and Reggie, each feeling very much abandoned, faced the brink of their destruction alone. Reggie ended a relationship which was destructive for him. He finally put his own self-care up front without reservation. At the same time, he believed deep down that Johanna wanted to be with him; that she was just as distressed about their problem as he was. He also knew that he wanted to work this out with Johanna, despite the sexual dilemma! Two needs guided him: he could no longer live in a destructive relationship and he would not live without sexual sharing. Reggie went to Johanna with his announcement.

Johanna listened but also held onto her own truth and self-interest. She let Reggie know she was unhappy too with the same issues and demonstrated a desire to find a resolution to their problems and stay together.

By luck or grace, the couple created a step they could take together. They could honor the other, and meet their own needs as well, without one feeling more damaged than the other in the process. They did not feel love, but they knew they still loved each other. In agreeing to this proposal, they confirmed in action their desire for mutuality: Reggie ended his participation in an unhealthy relationship and Johanna freed herself from Reggie's threats. These self-care measures lifted the couple from despair to new hope.

THE COMPARISON

It is tempting to create a false dichotomy between Meg's and Reggie's marital decisions. One might conclude that Meg abandoned her marriage by leaving Bill and Reggie sustained his commitment by staying with Johanna. This is simply not the case. Both Meg and Reggie left their "marriages;" Meg twice, and Reggie once. Meg left Bill the first time by placing self-care needs for physical survival above the need to care for Bill, made possible even with her low self-esteem by the responsibility she felt toward the care of the children. Bill's gambling addiction, with its tangential rages and other extreme actions, was harmful to them all. Therefore, she left Bill, physically; less so, emotionally. By leaving, Meg made clear to Bill her inability to place a higher value on regard for him or their marriage at the expense of herself and the children.

Meg paid a high emotional price for her self-care action. To leave Bill under these conditions negated all her beliefs about marriage. She had promised to "stand by him in all things, in sickness and in health." She could not continue to abide by a promise which was self-destructive. With enormous guilt, she left. It so happened that this move also forced Bill to clean up his act; and so he did. Meg then consented to return to Bill. For some time family life went well and she felt at peace, despite Bill's attempts to blame her for the temporary disruption of their family.

Meg vowed not to leave Bill again, unless forever. This vow entrenched Meg in a choking commitment to her old, intact notion of "marriage." Again, she subjugated the primacy of her legitimate self-interests to her husband's needs. It was only a matter of time before Meg would need to redress her commitment to this untenable arrangement.

In confronting her inner truth, Meg realized that she really did not want to be married to Bill no matter how clean his act. To fulfill her obligation to that vow made in emotional pain years before, Meg had to leave Bill *forever*. She became deathly ill under the curse of her self-imposed pledge. Her choices were few: die, but retain the old notion of commitment to Bill, or save her life and live with the consequences forever, which she did.

In much the same way, Reggie left his marriage. When he announced that he would no longer live in a sexless marriage, he left Johanna emotionally. It was as agonizing for him as for Meg with her decisions. Reggie placed his self-interests on the table. He left that part of his marriage which was toxic to him, the part that did not include his legitimate self-interests. No longer would he cooperate with a spouse who was hurting him. Like Meg, his self-interest had to take priority at this point. He too had previously placed the well-being of his spouse before himself. Reggie had privately endured his pain for years before he *said* he would leave. He acknowledged that his sexual needs were just as important to him as Johanna's needs were to her—to be supported, valued and loved in a way they each could recognize.

LOVEWORKS

Reggie's situation was somewhat different from Meg's. When he could acknowledge his pain to himself and say it out loud, he was freer than Meg to leave because he had not fused the idea of a committed relationship with suppression of his best interests. When he could name his pain, he was able to say, "I am leaving this relationship *as it is now constructed.* I can only stay if my legitimate interest in having a sexual relationship with you is honored in some fashion." Reggie broke out of his dilemma and changed his notion of marriage to Johanna. Whatever they chose next would include his well-being *and* Johanna's. In this way Reggie still honored marriage by staying open to a new step with Johanna.

Reggie ended a damaging relationship, promising himself a self-care component to relationship. He would no longer abandon his needs in the name of "marriage." Most importantly, he would not do anything without involving Johanna in the decision making process. In this way, Reggie kept his range of options wider than Meg had with her "endure everything or leave forever" vow. Reggie created a marriage with his spouse in which he could leave, come back, leave again, and do whatever he needed to develop a mutually acceptable plan with Johanna. Reggie's commitment to her had changed. It now included his own well-being as well as hers.

If Meg and Bill could have walked a few steps further along their path together, they may have also found a way to withstand the emotional divorce without the forces of guilt or anger burdening the already difficult process. The ultimate commitment is not to stay together at all costs. The goal is to hold each other in high enough regard, to maintain respect, to honor each other even here at this low point in their lives. This was the struggle Meg and Reggie shared. This is the struggle all men and women share when forming, sustaining, or leaving relationships.

In discussing these two couples and their struggles with each other, one might question the nature of their commitment to their partners. What is commitment? Many couples are confused about this term and fight over what they think the other's commitment should be. Often these days, young people choose not to marry because of a fear of what commitment implies. They are fearful of entrapment, of having their self lost or trampled.

COMMITMENT
When trying to define commitment, a useful approach is to ask: "Commitment to what?" Is marriage a commitment to an institution, some structure with an elaborate facade with no inner parts? Is it a commitment to a state of mind which demands that all feelings and longings be connected to one person only? Is the commitment to a person? If so, in what sense? Is it a commitment to live monogamously together? Or, is it a commitment to a oneness of purpose which forces the submission of individual truths, differing realities, and self-care?

Is the commitment to love? If so, in what sense? Is this love limited to feelings of love, which people cannot control, or another kind of love that goes beyond feelings?

Neither Meg nor Reggie could sustain a commitment to live with their chosen partners. Meg's understanding of commitment to a person left her needs out of the picture. There is no marriage if the price includes the loss of one of the selves. Reggie's sense of commitment allowed him to honor his partner's fear of losing him, helping him cope for a while until they could either agree to a plan of change or agree for him to leave the home.

Below is our understanding of marital commitment based upon equality:

1. Marital commitment must be to oneself first. Without a self one becomes lost. It is never the other's job to provide this self for anyone else.

2. Marital commitment is also to the other. The other needs to be valued and honored in his or her separateness. The other's wishes, desires, and needs are to be valued and addressed even if they are not mutual.

3. Marital commitment honors the simultaneous well-being of both spouses. No decision is complete until both agree. One person's need is not valued more than the other. They both hold equal value at all times on all issues. Dismissing and discounting a partner's desires when they are different is easy, but true marital commitment cannot tolerate such a mentality.

4. The honoring of both partners' well-being is lived out by committing to a *process* of decision making which serves the best interests of both spouses; not an easy task, but a simple concept. The two selves disagree fundamentally on a lot of issues. If the commitment to the process of mutual satisfaction is paramount, then negotiating does not stop until both are satisfied.

Reggie and Johanna agreed on the nature of the problem, their sexual dilemma. Another couple may disagree even here. The wife might take issue with her sexuality being singled out and name the husband's sports obsession as the central dilemma between them. If the commitment is to the well-being of both, then both definitions of the problem become valued and then dealt with. There is no contest here, only two persons who are in pain because of some actions of the other.

5. The vote on any marital issue is always a singular vote. One cannot speak for one's partner, but one needs to be separate enough to articulate one's needs and point of view. No discussion is complete without both parties' understandings on the table. Each needs to be able to cast a vote for a plan that includes the well-being of both. If there is no separateness, there can be no vote. If there is no vote, there can be no mutuality.

This outline explicitly defines the nature of a living commitment as dynamic, person-centered, and process-oriented. The commitment is workable and verifiable and has checks and balances of its own. A living commitment enables a marriage to be "big enough" for two equal partners.

A common belief is that men have difficulty making commitments. Men know they are reluctant to commit to a woman and usually feel awful about this problem down inside. They have a difficult time explaining their reticence to the woman as well as to themselves. Sometimes, it is not clear what women are asking of men on this issue. They want men to be permanently connected to them in some special way that is difficult to articulate, but powerful and very important. It feels like something a "commitment" would answer. But what is this commitment to? If this commitment is to maintain love-feelings, men will have trouble and, justifiably, will not commit.

A commitment made upon the basis of love-feelings is very difficult for men because their feelings are so closely tied to their sexuality. Men also know that their sexuality is threateningly promiscuous. Therefore, men are understandably reluctant to forsake all others when their sexual feelings run rampant and are inherently unreliable. Men must have more than love (sexual) feelings to stabilize themselves in a committed relationship. Their withholding a commitment is, in a way, protecting women from false pretenses. Men do not think they can be monogamous.

Men can, however, make a commitment to intimacy, especially if the contract contains the above conditions: a vote on all matters, honoring themselves and the women, and relying on a process between them as a couple which can handle the uncertainties of the male emotional life.

Men can make decisions and vote. They are used to being emotionally alone and can come to terms with a partner. But they have to stretch when consensus is understood to be the only acceptable decision. Men have to learn to break from their old win/lose orientation into a win/win; they *can* do this and must count on themselves to change.

The current chapter has highlighted the need for a redecision to commit to one another. For some, like Tom and Julie, this redecision is actually the first true decision about their new marriage made from their maturity. More decisions will follow.

In the next chapter, we will look at some other qualities both men and women must learn to assist them in their decision making, and we will return to Julie and Tom. They have arrived at the point of separateness and silently prepare for the next step. What they will decide at this point will make all the difference.

SECTION III
CHERISH

CHAPTER 9
"SECOND BEST"

Suggesting one settle for "second best" presents an auspicious beginning to the process of rebuilding a relationship. No one wants to *settle* for "second best" in anything, especially something so important as marriage. However, committing oneself to an intimate and equal partner necessitates a revision in how one *thinks* about what one wants.

"Second best" is the first choice to which both parties can agree and lend support without dishonoring themselves as individuals. This new option is really the new *first best* for their marriage and not "second best" at all. Settling for "second best" often connotes giving in or giving up. When couples bring the expectation to their marriages that they can get what they want, they always feel deprived when the reality hits that their partner does not want the same thing. They do not understand that "second best" for themselves is really the first best which is possible between them. There comes a time in every marriage where finding first best as a couple makes or breaks a relationship.

The process of choosing what path to follow is rooted in honor, fueled by the conflicting issue, and concluded with a new cherishing of each other. What does this mean? It means that each party will do nothing to violate self or the other. To violate, in this sense, is to superimpose one's value system, reality, or ideal solution on the other.

One couple was anticipating the birth of their first child. The husband watched a TV program about juvenile delinquency which disturbed him. He later told his wife that

99

she should not think about returning to work until their child was at least two years old. His wife, who was completing her doctorate and had an established career, did not take to this statement very well. She felt controlled, diminished, and not valued. This led to great anger, which was her outer manifestation of hurt and fear.

They were arguing about the child before it was even born! This couple had agreed to make all important decisions together, but this one the wife could not support. She spent considerable time arguing her case for part-time work beginning three to six months after the child's birth. The husband remained adamant against her working. The argument grew in intensity and volume. The wife was frustrated and frightened. She called a friend and relayed the details, expecting some compassion for her predicament. What she was told surprised her. The friend asked if she knew what her husband was really fighting for. "He wants our baby to be well cared for and to have a predictable and safe early environment," the wife said. Her friend then asked: "What do you want for your baby?" The wife, not yet realizing where this was going, said wailfully: "Well, I want the same thing for our child!" "Good," said the friend. "That's all your husband really wants to know. Do not get hung up on how many hours you can or cannot work while caring for a newborn. He wants to know that you find the child's needs paramount. As long as you both agree, you will honor each other in the choices. He cannot force you not to work if you want to do so. That will be your choice. But, if you both agree to the general needs of the child, then you will eventually negotiate how to carry them out."

The wife smiled. She had forgotten for a short while that she was in charge of her own values and that they would not evaporate if her husband disagreed with how these values would be expressed. He was coming from a different solution but he shared her values. She called her husband and told him she would do nothing with which ultimately he could not agree. She wanted him to participate in all decisions. She was thrilled that his attachment to their child commanded him to prepare for how it should begin life.

This couple will need to reach a "second best" conclusion at some point. The wife's first choices and the husband's first choices will conflict on this issue. Their decision to honor each other is the most important one, along with their willingness to give up what they each think is the very best way to raise a child. The real best way will be what they can put together as a couple. "Second best" for each will become the first best for the couple.

"Second best" is a difficult concept to comprehend fully. Reviewing the last few chapters may be helpful to understanding this concept.

Our couple, Tom and Julie, became incredibly disheartened in Chapter 6 when they felt deserted by each other. Their marriage left them feeling alone, abandoned, and forsaken. Neither could receive from the other the fulfillment they expected at the outset of their relationship.

In Chapter 7, they stood on some threshold and contemplated what to do next. From this vantage, they began some serious soul searching and discarded baggage they brought with them into marriage. They found themselves exposed to one another in their human frailty.

In Chapter 8, they searched for some new basis upon which to redecide their marriage. They were challenged to come to terms with their beliefs about themselves and the other. They found the guts to state the truth about what they wanted. Answering the question of whether to stay or leave, individually, they found the other was still present. They joined hands and stepped out together.

Now, in Chapter 9, they will take the first steps towards mutuality in their new union. Tom and Julie already have some experience with the concept of "second best." They have collaborated countless times without much thought, easily working towards an acceptable resolution to many disagreements. However, they have not yet understood "second best" as a *central concept of a good marriage* nor been able to apply it in their definition of relationship.

The following examples show the two required components for a second best choice: 1) achievable in real and measurable terms; and 2) mutually acceptable according to individual and joint values. This is the working definition of honor and a good working definition of commitment!

THE CAR

Tom and Julie bought a car a few years ago. They shopped around until they found their first choice, a magnificent car just the right color with the best horse power/fuel consumption ratio, fulfilling their image. The only problem with the vehicle was the high cost. For them to purchase their first choice they would have to give up their present home, something they were both unwilling to do. So they had to forego buying this dream car. With heavy hearts, they resumed their search. The next time they went to the showroom, they looked at cars in their price range to avoid setting themselves up again for disappointment. Their second best choice would really be the first best choice that was in reality possible for the couple to afford. They would be willing to "pay the price" for the second car, but not the first.

In a similar sense, Tom and Julie are disappointed about not being able to have their first best marriage. They are preparing for a "second best" marriage, if they can find how to make it work. Pursuing the marriage of their dreams was far too expensive in terms of emotional pain. They nearly killed themselves trying to bring into fruition the marriage they held in their own heads. Now they are looking for a different marriage, one that is "second best;" it is not the choice they would make if they had unlimited emotional resources. They must now create instead a relationship which is more respectful of each other, realizable, and respectful of their limited emotional endurance. At first, finding or creating this possible relationship is difficult. They have spent so much time and energy trying to obtain their first choice and spewing anger for not getting it, they have not given much thought to what else they might pursue.

Negotiating for "second best" is possible; negotiating for the first is not. It is too loaded with baggage: emotional issues from one's previous life, conflicting expectations of love, and idealistic fantasies promulgated by the culture. All these things blind people in marriage and set the stage for believing in a mirage. Prince and Princess Charming and Mr. and Mrs. Right do exist, but only in fantasy and film; one cannot negotiate for them. The "second best" exists in everyday life, rooted within the parameters of what the couple can create. But, "second best" must be found and be negotiated because no two people have the exact view of reality, priority of values, and taste. Unless one is married to a clone of oneself, differences will occur which must be honored to negotiate a mutually satisfying alternative.

The second quality of "second best," mutual acceptance, follows from the first. This requires patience. If it takes time to find the right car, it sometimes takes much more time to reach agreement on issues to which each brings a more personal investment (i.e., caring for a newborn).

THE NAME

When Tom and Julie named their first child, they presented their first choices to each other. To their chagrin, the other did not like any of their chosen names. They understood implicitly that the child would have a name to which they both agreed. The process they used during the months before the birth to reach agreement on a name was quite simple. They wrote down all their choices, threw out the ones they both disliked, and then looked at the pool of names left. From that list they found a name they both liked.

First best for the individuals gave way to "second best" and then some; but "second best" for the individuals became the first best for the couple.

Negotiating to a mutually acceptable conclusion is hard work. Couples are vulnerable to more acute, personal disappointment when they are forced to give up what is indispensable to their individual satisfaction. They remember the pain of relinquishing the indispensable items of love on the threshold, which they do not want to relive again. The old emotional problems have not gone away, and the couple does not trust their skill at this new task.

Tom and Julie, in particular, do not trust the other's ability to honor them. Tom still wants sex when Julie does not, and Julie wants Tom's attention when he does not want to give it. Both are still scared, hurt and angry. There is only one difference: They have crossed to the other side of the intimacy threshold. Here, they have their own truths and their own self-value, which are not negotiable! They do not need their partner's agreement to personal truths; they do not need to defend what they value before a critical gaze ever again. They need only hold to their truths without dishonoring each other: Tom loves Julie and has decided to do what he can to honor her even if Julie does not see his effort. Julie has decided the same. The significance of this commitment cannot be underestimated, allowing them an infinite range of possibilities for loving each other. They will soon find out.

THE BALL

Not long after Tom and Julie recommitted themselves to work through their impasses, opportunity knocked. Julie received an invitation to attend a formal ball to honor an important library benefactor and very good friend who was now retiring. The date, however, conflicted with a trip Tom had planned, and he was not willing to change his plans.

Julie was infuriated. As far as she was concerned, this was one more demonstration of Tom's unwillingness to devote any time to their relationship, occurring just after he agreed to work for mutuality with her in all things. She felt hurt by his decision and promptly fled to their bedroom for the rest of the afternoon, taking quite a long time to calm herself. Tempted to feel betrayed and to reinterpret his intentions, she stayed all night by herself, not showing her face until breakfast.

By morning, Julie had collected herself somewhat. She decided to talk with Tom who had been keeping his distance by spending time with the kids. First, she told him how she felt and that she was trying to believe his intentions, but it was hard. Then, she asked if he was willing to look at some options; he agreed.

Tom's intention was not to hurt Julie or prevent her from getting what she wanted. He simply was not willing to cancel this trip. He wanted to honor her as they had agreed, but honor his own needs as well. He knew she was upstairs very upset. He became angry at her, too, for shutting him out in a way that was so familiar to him, but he chose to wait and see. Tom realized he was not wrong in continuing his plans for the weekend even though Julie was hurt by his choice. In the past, he was very uncomfortable choosing for himself when Julie did not agree with his choice.

This time, Tom wanted the marriage to have a second chance, and he knew deep down inside that he had to respond differently for that to happen. He decided to trust Julie's ability to deal with her own reaction. He chose to give her some time to do that. When she asked to talk, he was very pleased he had held back his anger.

Several options occurred to them: 1) Julie could go with another escort; 2) she could stay home from the ball and give a special reception for her friend in her home at an earlier or later date with Tom committing to his presence and helping with the arrangements; or 3) Tom could look into changing his flight so he could attend the ball and still keep his weekend plans even though they would have to bear the additional expense of changing the tickets.

They probably could have created more options, but Julie actually liked the idea of a reception. She was attracted by the less formal atmosphere as well as the opportunity to spend more time with her friend than she would at the ball. Tom agreed wholeheartedly to support the reception plans with his time and effort. Julie was pleased.

THE COMMENTARY

Julie's pain was instant, deep, and congruent with the increased level of investment she had made in this relationship. She had to retreat for a while to be with herself. To her surprise, she felt a little better in the morning. This was a new experience. Heretofore, she gave into her anger, feeling better for the moment, but hating herself later on. This time she felt worse at first, but better later.

There will always be vestiges of the pain encountered when giving up some form of "the indispensable." These surface every time a partner looks after his/her own interest and serve as a reminder of sorts, as they learned at the threshold, that they are still quite alone in this relationship. To own and care for a separate self, they have to be alone, which is not a curse but a necessary component for intimacy. When they allow pain to have its place, whether because of an old wound which has been newly bruised, or because they feel alone when they do not want to, the pain will subside. The tasks are two: to resist the urge to convert one's discomfort into excessive anger or retaliatory behaviors; and to trust the other's intentionality manifested in the new redecision to deal with each other honorably.

The new marriage does not prevent pain. That would be an impossible contract. People feel strongly about those things they think are right or those things they want or value. Pain is inevitable when individual rights and values conflict.

In the new marriage, every negotiation hinges upon one very important competency. One must be able to say "no" in order to say "yes" and mean it. Spouses must be free to turn down the other's offer to prove to themselves that they are willing and able to look after their own interests in the negotiating process. Saying "no" is very, very difficult! Tom did not say "no" to Julie lightly. Actually, *saying* "no" is harder than *hearing* "no" because it goes against the intention to please the partner.

Having someone say "no" when you expected a wholehearted "yes" stings! Saying "no" and hearing "no" are important maturing experiences. They instill confidence to say "yes" and mean it while still honoring themselves. More importantly, the "yes" can be trusted as a real and true "yes" with no hidden discord. Spouses can now willingly say "yes" to a proposal which seems promising and their partners will be able to trust them. The commitment will no longer be questioned.

When "no" is announced, the partner often feels the hurt which they experience as rejection, along with emotional vestiges of the hurt connected to bothersome roots of "the indispensable." But the pain is not the same. The new twitches of pain, when they occur, are not experienced quite as powerfully and will not last as long as the pain endured when giving up "the indispensable." Since both partners have already been through the worst at the threshold, risking another "no" about something less important may hurt but will not be as painful.

When men put forward their proposals, they generally think the woman's "no" is unjust. After all, they have spent a good deal of time thinking through what they wanted which seemed logical and reasonable.

Women, when their proposals are declined, feel deprived and devalued since they spend so much time deferring to others' needs. To have someone so special negate their plans on one of the rare times they ask for something is extremely painful. Screaming, "You're being unfair!" or "I'm unimportant to you!" will not get couples what they want. They simply have to accept their partner's "no" and negotiate some more. The willingness to look for something else, in spite of bruised feelings, takes work, but is necessary. Walking the first few steps is always the most difficult. However, they are not as strenuous as trying to make the old marriage work.

One can think of saying "no" as the pruning of a fruit tree which, done properly, will increase the harvest. Some branches we let grow. These are the "yes's." Some parts we cut off; these are the "no's." Yes's and no's, separate votes taken together, are the tools for building a mutually satisfying relationship. The more one *uses* them, the richer the harvest. The first few successes come quite hard, but nothing succeeds like success. One builds upon the other. In the end, a new appreciation and fondness grows for the partner who trusts the process, trying to build the next step. In this way, couples learn to cherish their partners.

Tom and Julie have been in suspended animation on the threshold of intimacy for a long time. Tom now offers Julie his hand. He is willing to go forward if she is. Julie, now the reticent one, considers carefully her response. She does not trust Tom, but at some level she realizes her trusting him is not important. The real questions are: Can she trust herself to look after her own interests and can they take a step together which will honor their respective needs and

yet address their issues? They have come clean with what
they want from each other and revealed the soft underbelly
of vulnerability. Their hurt at each other's hands is obvious.
Can they find a way to deal with themselves and the other on
all kinds of issues?

Julie thinks Tom is unavailable to her except when
he wants sex. Tom thinks Julie cannot be pleased no matter
what he does or does not do. He believes she values him
only for what he provides in support to the family. They
have tried to change all this without success. Do they each
have to give up on what they most want? Do they have to
settle for "second best" in everything?

Julie and Tom are no different than most couples.
The desires of their hearts are not being realized in their marriage. The continued effort to bring them into fruition is
futile and often more damaging. They are ready, although
they do not like the idea of shifting gears, to find that which
might be realizable.

Men do not usually value second place. They like to
win. Men like Tom think they are losing if they do not win.
Second place feels like last. Tom must learn to value
something he can have with Julie in spite of how he feels.

Julie has had much experience in accepting less than
what she wants. As a woman, she has put herself on the
back burner many times. Julie has come to the end of that
road. She wants *what* she wants *when* she wants it: now!
And she cannot have her way, especially now. Julie must
deal with her choices to defer to the family needs during past
years and separate that from the need to find "second best"
with Tom now. Intuitively, Julie knows what is being asked
of her in this new arrangement.

Julie takes Tom's outstretched hand. The change in
Julie and Tom is subtle; they have ceased being enemies and
now have joined forces toward a common goal, finding a
move they can take. Together in spirit if not on all individual
first bests, they prepare for the next step.

CHAPTER 10
THE COST OF EQUALITY

When men and women stretch out their hands to each other inviting a new beginning, they must prepare themselves for individual maturing. They must know and then speak their own truth for on-going self-care, and they must be able to hear their partner's attempts to do the same. This isn't always easy. The other's truth can touch old wounds which still smart and ooze without warning. Simple factual comments may feel negative. Neither wants to threaten the peace with negativity; peace cannot endure unless the negatives are addressed . . . soon. What do they do?

Couples hope the honesty they share "alone together" on the intimacy threshold will be a one-time activity, that they will not have to repeat the process on a regular basis. Many couples reveal in crisis that which they routinely withhold when life returns to normal. This is a problem.

The intimate and equal marriage expects negatives. Its members become increasingly less apprehensive of unwanted consequences and more available to the value of not having to pick and choose what will and will not offend a mate. Even though they occasionally feel stung by the other's words, each occasion presents the opportunity to decide to feel wounded and focus on self or to focus on the partner's issue which he/she is trying to express.

Ed, considering a fresh start on his relationship with his wife, proposed they research moving into a less expensive home. Margie refused. Ed was devastated because he thought she might welcome a fresh start. Margie's counterproposal, to separate their monies while still living together, met with an equally adamant "no" from Ed. They stepped back again and looked at each other. Would this become a battle of wills or would they be able to receive each other's negative response without bringing the quality of the other's loving into the ring?

Strands of "the indispensable" infiltrate every step along the way. At this junction, couples are prone to engage love and marriage as allies to their causes. "If you really loved me, you would not hurt me or make me feel sad. You would know this is important to me and back off." Or one might try: "If this marriage were important to you, you would not put yourself first, you would not cause conflict, and you would not say 'no' so often."

Each is still testing the other with the only measuring stick they know: whether or not the other loves them enough in their own unique brand of love. To form the new rela- tionship, a measuring stick based upon self-care must be created which receives "no" and "yes" with a new eye, a new ear, and responds to conflict in a different voice. Two selves need to be honored in the marriage.

WOMEN: COMING OUT

Women often resist taking their place in the intimate and equal marriage for several reasons. First, some women defer to men's wishes in order to protect and further the rela- tionship. This handicaps women in negotiating intimacy with men. Also, the thought of having to negotiate for self in the marriage violates their definition of love.

Women also have problems saying "no" because the definitive nature of the word misses the complexity inherent in most issues. Women are tuned in to a wide range of details surrounding problems. Most issues are not resolvable for them with a simple "no" or "yes." Third, saying "no" establishes a firm boundary, emotionally separating women from those they love. Because connecting is so valuable and fundamental for women, their relationships feel threatened by hard and fast boundaries, particularly the saying "no" kind. Surely, there's a way to work things out!

Lastly, women do not want to alienate those they love by being uncooperative, unsupportive, or selfish. Being helpful, available, and self-sacrificing is very import- ant to them. Saying "no" limits the scope of love's generos- ity and forces women to identify and care for their own needs as part of loving. But . . . saying "no" minimizes the tendency to turn needs into demands later on.

These problems with saying "no" put women at a seeming disadvantage when negotiating for "second best"

110

choices. Their growth into an intimate and equal relationship will command them to become more definitive about self-care, to redefine boundaries, and to expand their options.

To form their part of an intimate and equal marriage, women will need to make choices for self from a more positive and less reactive stance. Men need to know this is not an easy process for women. To generously put themselves out when someone they love has a need is second nature to women. They cannot comprehend why men are not wired together the same way.

THE COUPLE: TURNING AROUND

Men have a different orientation to the saying "no" saga. Decisions are readily made. Their natures predispose them to be able to say "yes" and "no" more readily, which they do daily at work. They must look out for number one.

However, men have difficulty in taking their place in an intimate and equal relationship, too. For one, they are not as fine-tuned to their own needs as women. Men often "miss" emotional pulls and concerns until the pulls become huge. Men feel handicapped in negotiations with women when they do not know what they need, and most men do not know what they need in this newly emerging "second best" relationship. They clam up, go away, or dominate, often to cover up their loss for words to describe their needs. Furthermore, men do not want to admit they even have needs because they do not want to put themselves into a position of vulnerability. Having a need means one might have to do without. Men do not like being so vulnerable. This goes against every male cell in their bodies.

Here is an irony. Women think they know what is good for the relationship but are less able to negotiate. Men think they are able to negotiate but are less clear about what will make things better. Men and women need each other to accomplish the task at hand. Gender related predispositions affect them both.

Tom and Julie share this dilemma with other men and women. They must now choose to learn a new skill that seems contrary to their natures. Julie has to develop the capacity to say a decisive "no" to what Tom wants. She must emotionally risk the relationship in order to place herself into the negotiating mode. Tom must learn to read his internal world better to know what emotional needs he must bring to the bargaining table and be willing to do so.

Both spouses face private fears as they enter the negotiation process. They each feel disadvantaged, certain the other has an easier task ahead. Tom might be tempted to think the task for Julie is more simple than for him. After all, she only has to say "no" to something she already has ideas about. Julie might be tempted to minimize Tom's long and arduous task, accustomed as she is to hearing him speak his mind readily. But the emotional toll to think and act differently is equally traumatic for both.

MEN: GOING INSIDE

The internal world men avoid must be faced, but it threatens them. Going inside challenges their perceived maleness and seems contrary to a primary quality. Men think they are supposed to be warriors, protectors, wage earners, and successful. They know they are limited, but admitting to limitations seems to violate a prevailing male code which says, "Don't let anyone know you are limited!" In a man's competitive world, one does not reveal one's vulnerabilities to one's opponent. She might be able to destroy him! Even men who are open-minded and gentle leave this area of growth at the bottom of the list.

Men will resist the intimate and equal marriage by pretending an inner world does not exist until the anger they feel requires an explanation. What's happening for men? Looking at these men from the outside, they appear confident, busy, and preoccupied with their own interests. They seem self-absorbed or selfish, in a bad sense of the word.

On the inside, they pay little attention to themselves except every once in a while when they feel depleted. At those moments, they are likely to grab a mental health day, play golf, and then come home after a few beers ready to make love. Again, looking upon them from the outside, they appear even more selfish, self-centered, and self-absorbed.

Women understandably find men unreachable, shallow, and self-centered. Even more understandable is that men do not have a clue why women feel the way they do about them. Men's subjective experience does not match the information coming from the women. Worse, men believe what the women say, more than they believe their own insides. Many men feel guilty about making their women unhappy. In response, they double their efforts in playing husband, father, and wage earner. They also become more desperate for sex and golf, which in turn distresses their wives. Round and round they go. The negative feelings build inside but are ignored.

Early in relationships men easily say things from the heart women want to hear. Expressing feelings is effortless for a while, especially when they are so positive. Women and men both know this ease does not last. Life's routines, increased pressure at work, and family responsibilities return men to a strong problem solving mode. Secured by the love of a woman, men turn their attentions to their roles. Here, men focus on the outside world and guard closely their internal world, keeping themselves safe to fight yet another working day. More and more, they ignore the inside in service of competing better in the world.

Men eventually notice negative feelings because felt violation and anger are attached; these they recognize. When these feelings are connected to the women they love, men are uncomfortable. Negative feelings threaten the status quo. They do not want to rock the boat. Therefore, men ignore bad feelings as long as possible. When men finally try to deal with their feelings, they have great difficulty.

Men miss the mark with feelings for three reasons. First, men have difficulty discerning the difference between a feeling and a behavior in the real world. When men *feel* like they have done something wrong, they believe they *have* done something wrong. When men are unhappy on their jobs, they conclude they need new ones. When they are attracted to someone, they must do something. Sadly, when men do not *feel* love for their wives, they hastily conclude love is gone.

113

This inability to distinguish between feelings and behaviors in the real world leads men to suppress them. The consequence of acknowledging them is terrifying since feelings are perceived as being true. Better to suppress them and maintain the marriage! Pressure builds until one day they feel overwhelmed. When men reach this boiling point, they can no longer survive in a marriage containing all these negative feelings. They do not feel love. One day, they come home from work and tell their wives they have decided they are not in love anymore. They pack their bags and leave! Integrity requires they act on what they feel. To *feel* the feeling, report it, and *let it be* simply does not occur to them.

With such turmoil bubbling under the surface, men only have a portion of themselves available for marriages after a time. They suppress the negative stuff which they believe will cause trouble and use up all the positive stuff early. They become the best husbands possible under the circumstances. Underneath ticks a time bomb. When women feel like their men are not really connected to them, they are right. An increasing portion of the husband's self is not being expressed in the marriage but lies dormant somewhere deep inside, growing with intensity by the day.

Second, men do not realize that feelings, while important, change, especially after being expressed. Feelings rarely change, however, without expression. The fact that men hide feelings from themselves, as well as from women, ingrain these negative feelings into a permanent fixture on their souls. In reality, feelings change almost as soon as the words leave the lips. Men do not know this.

Third, men do not know they are not responsible for feelings. One cannot be held accountable for a feeling, no matter what it is. Men are accountable for what they do, not what they feel. Feelings exist in a world of their own, as do thoughts and beliefs. Men do not know this. Men feel like they are personally responsible for everything that "goes bump in the night." Men torment themselves with unwanted thoughts and feelings for which they hold themselves mercilessly responsible.

LOVEWORKS

Most of men's concerns center around their sexuality because they tend to sexualize their feelings. Coupling this sexual preoccupation with men's poor understanding of feelings, the stage is set for affairs of the imagination or affairs in reality.

Men seem to think that just because they can fantasize an exciting sexual experience with other women, they do not really care for their chosen partner as they think they should. Fantasizing must mean they *love* the other woman more. Trouble begins. Men think they are untrue to their partners just because they feel attracted to another. They must not be good mates. Oh, the guilt!

Some men are secretly ashamed of what goes on in their heads. Others play "devil be damned" and act out on everything. Either way, men are disparaging of their own sexual selves. Perhaps this explains their extreme defensiveness when women accuse them of being overly preoccupied with sex. It takes a long time for a man to learn that fantasies are not necessarily saying anything at all about them, except that they are sexual beings. Verbalizing this layer of feelings is a vulnerable experience for men.

Men are incredibly dependent on their relationship with women for their sexual identities, "to feel like men." Needing more support than they received from fathers in their early years and barely surviving the daily assaults to masculinity at the work site, men look to their women for feelings of value. Men are in a bind. Not wanting to risk further estrangement from their women whose support is vital, they withhold information which they feel may threaten this relationship. They lie; they omit; they hide and deny. All in the name of relationship! Men prefer to distance themselves rather than give credence to and then talk about what they think they are not supposed to feel inside. Whatever connection men have to their mates must be guarded at all costs. Hence, silence.

Keeping secret this negative information alienates men further. The "Catch 22" is awesome. The part of themselves attached to negative feelings must withdraw from the relationship, and the women will know something is wrong.

115

Eventually men realize they cannot win. Since women loath the silent distancing man, negativity is created anyway. Trying to avoid negativity brings it on. Only when men begin to feel there is no way out do they become ready to address their internal worlds.

But the fear of untold consequences to dealing with feelings takes its toll on men's relationships. There is no escape from this fear. Nevertheless, they must move on, not so much to preserve the relationship, but more to become whole. Taking this personal stand is absolutely necessary if men are to find peace.

The fact that men are calling all the cards when they begin to speak cannot be understated. They leave themselves more vulnerable than at any other time in their lives. Yet they must do it. Men, facing themselves and their intimate others, reach the ultimate pain, being unacceptable in their partner's eyes. When men tell their spouses about themselves, they risk rejection. Men feel like their masculinity is at stake.

Both fortunately and unfortunately, men finally come to the end of this road. Men now are forced to define themselves separately from women and their partner's view of them. When they do, they find they survive. They form a new definition of themselves no one can take away. From this point of freedom, men will no longer need to be dependent on women, on a job, or on anything external, to feel like men. This represents the maturity necessary to begin to be intimate.

THE REWARDS

Couples approach the intimate and equal marriage with differing strengths. Women are more capable of intimacy but struggle to claim their equal places. Men are more capable of standing up for themselves yet struggle with their inner selves, the heart of intimacy. When both men and women acknowledge the negatives, they are actually solidifying their own identities independent from the partner. They become whole by facing each other. They are now secure enough to stand face to face, ready to negotiate: women armed with a "no," the men armed with their needs.

Yes's and no's, separate votes taken together, are the prerequisites for building a mutually satisfying relationship. The more one speaks one's own truth, the easier it becomes. The first few successes come quite hard, but again, nothing succeeds like success. In the end, a new appreciation and fondness grows for the partner who stays with the process of finding the next step. Couples begin to cherish their partners.

The cost of equality is the price of our sexual identities. Women need to redefine their femaleness apart from nurturing relationships, and men need to redefine their maleness apart from pleasing females.

The cost of equality is also the emotional price paid for growing up and becoming whole, for becoming independent, and for needing each other less to buttress self-esteem. We rail against our own integration in the name of relationship until we cannot anymore. Women, at their wits end, stand up and count themselves important, giving up the chase. Men, exhausted from avoiding loneliness and fear, stop rationalizing their choices and listen to their feelings.

Men and women let go and face their fears, rather than continue the stranglehold on the other. This is the price they each pay for giving up their unique ways of avoiding growth.

Facing fears is not a high cost, as life goes. No one dies from going where they have feared to go. The self-discoveries are at least empowering and usually freeing. The fruits are plentiful.

Most surprising of all, those who stay with this exacting process find a personal sense of accomplishment. They did it! They did not give up and are very proud of themselves. No one can ever diminish the fruits of the journey, and this makes all the difference. An inner stability prepares them to learn to negotiate.

LOVEWORKS
CHAPTER 11
NEGOTIATING LOVE

Although Tom and Julie think they are now ready to negotiate a "second best" relationship, more preparatory work looms ahead. They still need to reorganize their thinking about love and hone existing skills to maneuver the recurring disappointments. They naively believe that surrendering their dream marriage completes the hard work. Not yet. Relinquishing the ideal paves the road they must now walk awkwardly together. There are four more immediate decisions to be made individually for the negotiating process to bear fruit: 1) reconsidering "the indispensable;" 2) overcoming the resistance to negotiate love; 3) facing conflict; and 4) accepting the price of vulnerability.

We contend the purpose of modern marriage is to realize intimacy. Also, the deeper levels of intimacy men and women crave must flow from equality between the spouses. We believe men and women are not sufficiently emotionally evolved to bring into fruition that which they seek. Herein lies the problem and the possibility! Maturation roots will deepen in everyone as they progress toward intimacy. Ironically, men and women need each other to develop into this greater maturity. It is a chicken/egg scenario. They need the maturity to be intimate but they need the intimacy (the proximity to each other) to develop the maturity.

Soon Tom and Julie will recognize they need each other to foster the stretching of self that cannot happen in isolation. This realization will put their decision to seek "second best" solutions in a better light. Being with each other will force them to choose to deal with the four issues listed. These areas become problematic for couples who think they have already accomplished the tasks. They know they have agonized their way through these subjects before and resist feeling the pain of letting go of their ideals again. But these subjects are like the trick birthday candles which do not extinguish. What does extinguish the flames? Actually, they burn themselves out over time. That is the raw but golden truth about the issues below. Tom and Julie will find intimacy with each other if they can sustain trust through some painful choices over and over again. The willingness, or not, to work through these crucial areas of sensitivity, described below, decides the fate of many marriages.

THE HAUNTING INDISPENSABLE

Vestiges of desiring "the indispensable" remain very much alive in both Tom and Julie. Of course, they will feel let down again by the other, and they will feel angry and hurt. One wrong sigh or turned back can, in an instant, return them to feeling alone, together. Despite protestations to the contrary, a flame of hope lingers in all our hearts for love the way we want it. So what is it? We all want to realize approval, find unconditional love, feel secure and included, receive justice and countless other human needs which were inadequately addressed when we were children. We want partners to make up for our losses and repair our wounds. Maybe they can and, sometimes, they do. When the desire becomes an unacknowledged subtle but indispensable demand, it must then burn itself out over time with much gentleness. If the couple is still sensitive to old pulls, the system will remain quite fragile during this letting go time. In that atmosphere, it is easy to *feel* like nothing is changing. Patience with oneself and one's partner is mandatory.

NEGOTIATING LOVE

Tom and Julie will find the very act of having to negotiate for love offensive. They think they should just receive it, not have to bargain for it. They think the magic is broken when love becomes constant choices. An unwritten book of love taught to all at some ripe and tender age promises love will come to everyone for no reason. If Tom and Julie have to bargain for love, it is easy to think it is not love at all.

Julie truly values a half hour after dinner alone with Tom to talk over the day. When he is available, she really feels loved. To ask Tom for this time (and negotiate how long and how often) feels like a contract rather than love. Dealing with this issue feels contrived. In Julie's frame-

LOVEWORKS

work, the loving gesture, i.e., Tom's presence to her after dinner, is only love if he offers it because he has intuited she wants it or because he wants it, too.

A great deal of time and maturity are required to appreciate the benefits of the new partnership, i.e., attaining larger doses of pleasure more often because it is not left to mind reading. The price is exacting . . . giving up the magic of relationships "happening" all by themselves.

Negotiating love is a daily activity. Negotiating only the ultimate terms of a relationship is not enough. Everything that occurs throughout the day is potential for the negotiating table. This is grueling work, especially in the beginning, when love-feelings are again in jeopardy with this decision making process. Mundane issues . . . who will wash the dishes, when to get together for sex, how much money to spend on a sofa, how she spoke to him when she walked into the room, how she felt when he yelled at the kids . . . may be on the table on any given day.

CONFLICT

Tom and Julie are afraid conflict will threaten their newfound, rocky stability. It is tempting to overlook things which bother them, to defer to the other's wishes when not wanting to, and to desist in asking for things needed. Conflict feels bad and goes against another unwritten rule to which we ascribe that says conflict *is* bad. To choose to allow conflict when it is there anyway, to let a spouse feel hurt and/or angry for a time, and to risk the marriage by sharing one's needs and feelings out loud is not bad at all. These choices can *save* a damaged relationship.

This is a very hard choice for both Tom and Julie. Their marriage eroded because they did not know how to speak out to each other. Tom hated to see Julie cry; Julie hated to risk Tom's going further away. In the end, Julie cried a lot anyway and Tom went far away. Bad feelings cannot be avoided. Allowing conflict will actually save time and pain.

Conflict does not have to be brutal or deadly. If Tom and Julie can accept this new truth, they will continue to talk to each other, and conflict will be less and less onerous. Hence, at some point they must say to each other, "I do not like this, can we look at another possibility?" In the beginning, the "I do not like this" part is conflict and challenges the other in a way which upsets the status quo. But after awhile, it becomes useful information, especially as they improve at "looking at another possibility."

VULNERABILITY

Negotiating for what Julie and Tom want will force them to become more vulnerable to each other. Staying tuned in to their own needs, wants, and feelings, they will, of course, have to share them out loud more often. When a spouse says from a vulnerable place, "I am really excited about learning to play the piano; I have wanted to do this all my life," and the partner scoffs and laughs, a person can feel stung and perhaps rejected. Deciding to make an issue about something relatively trivial takes effort and calls forth more vulnerability. But, if a spouse cannot talk about small embarrassments, how will this person ever be able to say to his/her spouse, "I would enjoy our lovemaking so very much more if you could brush your teeth (or look me in the eyes, or allow the light to be on, etc., etc.)." Very intimate issues only emerge in safety. Choosing to risk vulnerability is the first step in getting needs met with each other. These areas are very tender. Lingering fear of exposure and rejection tempt one to remain silent and the other to retaliate. Couples will tend to take honest differences personally. It will feel like, "Here is my weak spot, hit me if you have to."

Each of the above areas involve decisions to remain with a new process leading to intimacy. Couples will choose to be on guard for the trick candle of "the indispensable," the recurring resistance to negotiating love, the tendency to avoid conflict, and the price of vulnerability. The new marriage of equal, intimate partners will continue to include hard decisions by each partner. These choices were not necessarily a prerequisite when intimacy and equality were not shared priorities. Couples only have to deal with themselves in these new ways because they are trying to

LOVEWORKS

create an intimate marriage between two equals.

EASY-TO-LEARN SKILLS[1]

If Tom and Julie are still walking the walk after reviewing the above, they have access to some easy-to-learn skills which will make the trek more pleasant. Just as one must have special tools to repair an engine or special equipment to climb a mountain, so too must Tom and Julie cultivate unique abilities to be able to negotiate.

AN ABSOLUTE COMMITMENT
TO A WIN/WIN OUTCOME

The beauty of negotiating with an intimate and equal partner is that a win/win outcome is possible, honoring both partners. A wife can plan a three week vacation in her head, then offer it to her husband as a *fait accompli*, only to be surprised by his negative response. In a win/win system, he can tell her his concerns, and she can promise him that absolutely no itinerary will be made until they can both agree to the choices. As Tom and Julie come to appreciate the fact that the other will work for a mutual solution, they will be less inclined to react with anger, less inclined to "protect" their turf, and less inclined to place their own well-being over the other.

ASK FOR WHAT IS REALLY WANTED

Because Tom and Julie are vulnerable to each other, it is tempting to skirt sensitive issues through omission of valuable information or lead with indirect questions. Somehow, they avoid asking for what they really want as a way to protect their true vulnerable needs. Tom and Julie are doing their emotional best to acknowledge and honor the spoken request. When one asks for something of secondary importance and the other finds out later what was really wanted, the avoiding spouse contributes to the partner's feeling

[1] Several of these skills are described in Fisher, Robert and Ury, William, *Getting to Yes: Negotiating Agreement Without Giving In*, Penguin Books,1991, pages 17-94.

122

LOVEWORKS

deceived, angry, or hurt. He/she resents not being dealt with directly. The respondent will feel justifiably used, and, worse, will not receive credit for his/her cooperation because he/she has not responded to the real need. One might as well come out with the truth in the beginning. It almost always comes out in the end anyway. Indirectness muddies the waters!

NEVER AGREE TO SOMETHING YOU ARE NOT PREPARED TO DO

Tom and Julie can cause trouble by making promises they really cannot keep. Fearful of conflict, they may not say "no" when they really need to. One or the other will await the fulfillment of an agreement, only to feel angry days or weeks later because the promise was not realized. This can be quite a problem because the fragile new threads of trust are weakened by these actions. "Yes" means "yes" to an activity, event, or project, not "I love you." "No" means "no" to an activity, event, or project, not "I do not love you." The couple needs to take a deep breath and let each other say the truth that is there to say. Better to say "no" than "yes" and not follow through.

DO NOT OFFER GIFTS NOT ASKED FOR AND EXPECT ACCOLADES

Tom and Julie, like most people, knock themselves out offering gifts to each other they think the other might want but never request. Tom gave Julie a set of golf clubs one year for her birthday. She played golf a little, but Tom never quite felt appreciated enough for this great gift. Julie gave Tom a massage one year and he actually became angry at her. Birthday, holiday, and special occasion presents are replete with the interests which please the giver more than the receiver. This version of offering only the love which exists in one's own head finds Tom and Julie guilty as charged. They forget that their partner's differentness demands the cultivation of listening skills to hear accurately the other's desires. Couples become locked in on what they think their partners like. People change. Desires change.

123

LOVEWORKS

Exhausting themselves in areas which are unappreciated by the other diminishes their ability to extend themselves in new areas which are extremely important to the other. They must check things out explicitly before making an offer and not feel offended if the spouse says "No, thanks." If the intention is to please, receiving clear information about what is wanted will be very helpful.

AVOID PSEUDO-COMPROMISE

A true compromise makes each partner feel good. They each gain some of what they want. Many couples, Tom and Julie included, think they make compromises all the time. In truth, they often agree to some plan simply to end conflict or avoid potential conflict.

For example, Tom and Julie each anticipated a wonderful Saturday evening together. Tom wanted to sink into a sofa with Julie and watch a movie. He thought Julie would like this too, but Julie was exploring restaurant guides. She very much wanted to have a long candlelight dinner with Tom in an elegant setting. The dilemma is familiar to many couples on many Saturday nights. How do they compromise? Tom and Julie at first decided to cancel both the rental movie and the dinner out because neither wanted to do what the other wanted. They thought about going for a walk and some fast food, a pseudo-compromise. Neither would have been happy. Then they considered Tom's plan, but Julie would have been very disappointed. They tried on Julie's option, but Tom was very tired and really wanted to wear jeans and relax.

Pseudo-compromises become live options when plans do not gel easily. Each suggests several ideas to which the other turns up a nose. Annoyance creeps in; the intimacy slips to the back burner as the couple nitpicks over the activities. Sometimes these episodes end with one person saying, "Whatever you want, dear" or "I do not care." That is a deadly ending, guaranteed to produce a tedious pseudo-compromise. Often the couple does nothing for the evening. They stay home together out of some search for the right answer and lose an opportunity for real goodness.

Pseudo-compromises do not advance the issue or their relationship. They only succeed in ending the discussion and the intimacy!

IDENTIFY CONCERNS

Let us continue with Tom and Julie and their Saturday night dilemma. They must lighten their grip on their mutually exclusive positions to understand why the proposed activities were chosen. In this way, they identify what interest or concern the proposed solution has handled.

Here is the brass ring. There are always concerns which lie behind all couples' attempted solutions. Acknowledging the legitimacy of the other's concerns, even if they do not comprehend, let alone agree, honors the other and also lays the groundwork for addressing the concern. In so doing, both will feel valued, even if they do not do what they had desired to do in the first place.

Tom and Julie talked. Julie was feeling distant from Tom and wanted him all to herself in a special way; hence, the dinner out. Tom was feeling in need of getting as close to Julie as he could for as long as he could. The movie seemed like a good vehicle for snuggling. He was feeling weary and empty. Her love could replenish him. Aha! They wanted, in this instance, the same thing with each other. They just had different plans for getting there. Settling for a damaging pseudo-compromise would have ultimately deprived them of the sharing they each desired. Each needed to identify their true concern, no matter what the other did with it. When their interests were appreciated, the true compromise emerged. He needed to be home and snuggle; she needed to be fed in a special setting while enjoying conversation with Tom. So, Tom cooked while Julie set an elegant table. They ate, talked, and snuggled. Not all compromises are so easy to settle. But the process is similar for even difficult issues.

Earlier in the text, we mentioned a couple who fought over how soon the wife should go back to work after the birth of their first child. The couple resolved the issue when they found their common denominator, the ultimate well being of their child. Rather than having to fight about whether the wife would go back to work in four weeks or four months, they could rest for a while in the shared value of their child's emotional development. It was not a power play after all, as they had each interpreted. Actually, they agreed on giving their child the best home possible but disagreed somewhat on how to provide it. For now, they agreed to table the discussion on how each of them would be present to the child. They feel better because they know they share the same value. The ultimate solution would be worked out at a later date. Identifying their concerns moved them along. This example also demonstrates the following seventh negotiating skill.

JOIN FORCES AGAINST THE PROBLEM

How quickly couples make each other the enemy when conflict occurs. In our story, neither Tom nor Julie, nor either of the potential parents, is the problem. The real problem is the irresolution of the difficulty. If the couples can join together to defeat their common problem, their energies will be much better utilized. Of course, it is clear they will do less damage to each other in the process. It is also clear that problems can be solved. Love is not on the line, marriage is not on the line, egos are not on the line . . . only a problem. The unique gifts they each bring to their marriage can join together to deal with problems.

STAY WITH THE PROBLEM

We have already mentioned this in another section, but it is worthy of repetition. Most couples give up (or give in) way too soon. Sticky strands of the old indispensable intrude on the present even when couples try to honestly state the problems. Stating the problems calmly and respectfully does not mean that the other will acquiesce to one's choice. The new first best is always the desired goal.

Even if Tom and Julie agree to look for what is in second place, it does not mean the second proposal will become the new first best. Rejection of the second offer may hurt almost as much as the first. An infinite number of options are available to the couple if they continue to stay with the problem. Identifying concerns remains paramount. Rejected offers are not signs of waning love, merely of a different reality. Each needs to retain their own truths and stay open to the other. They *will* find something mutually acceptable. This agreed upon option will finally represent the next first step of their new relationship.

TOM AND JULIE

The following anecdote helps us close our study of Tom and Julie. They indeed evolved through several stages of their new marriage and were happy. The new peace felt good. Old love-feelings returned; they relaxed their guard and became prime candidates for a new incident! How they handled the "incident" is telltale of their progress.

One night, Tom noticed that Julie was taking longer than he expected to complete a shopping trip. He had come home early, planned and cooked dinner, then waited for her return. While he was in the shower, Julie called and left a message on the answering machine announcing a delay of an hour or so. "Go ahead and eat without me," she said. But Tom did not check for messages for an hour, during which time he began to stew. After he heard the message, he felt disappointed, but received the news well enough. When one hour became two, he felt antsy, agitated, and then, angry!

Julie arrived home happy. She found some great bargains. She felt pleased to take the time she needed, believing that she and Tom were well connected and he would understand. Love burst inside her. In her head, Julie planned a wonderfully romantic evening with Tom upon her return.

When Julie entered the house, Tom was aloof. Julie asked him several times if there was a problem. He finally told her he was angry. She felt hit by a baseball bat in the gut. Love-feelings vanished on a dime! She reconnected to a fear that had long gripped her: "I cannot really be myself with him. The consequences are too painful to endure. It is not safe to love. I am always hurt."

The couple talked after a while and reached an

uneasy peace. Then Julie withdrew emotionally. Tom felt even angrier! Tom promptly withdrew behind his "I can handle anything, but I am really not here" screen.

After a few days of interacting functionally, they missed each other. Each waited for the other to "come back first." This did not happen. What did happen was the result of coming to know themselves better across the intimacy threshold. They had faced each other at least once before with their painful truths and the results had been valuable. This memory freed them to talk about the lack of intimacy and discuss how they could reestablish the warmth between them.

To regain trust, they reviewed the painful week, including the incident. Neither wanted to go over the events, but they did so anyway and *heard* for the first time the other's story. Each was right; no one was wrong. Both had been caught up briefly in an indispensable pull: "He/she should receive me the way I am, lovingly, and without negative reaction. To me, negative reaction means non-love and I have to change. I had better leave this relationship to protect myself."

After the couple talked, compassion for the other's dilemma surfaced. They still felt bruised but less indicted and more aware of their own interpretations of the other than before. They felt hopeful. Most of all, they realized how capable they were of reading each other's words and actions negatively. They could still believe without much reflection that the other might intend to wound, diminish, and thwart. How quickly they had contemplated separating; how quickly they concluded life would not work with each other; how blind they could still be to the larger picture in any given moment.

For Tom and Julie, the intimate and equal marriage they desired became more and more possible each time they resolved problem situations in a respectful way. They accepted conflict, kept the value of their selves intact, and did not put the marriage on the line. They had learned to trust the process, trust the process, trust the process—a process which would be repeated time and time again over the years.

The difference now, though, is that they *know how* to improve their relationship, they have the necessary tools, and they have experienced success as they continue building a more intimate and equal marriage.

CHAPTER 12
INTIMATE AND EQUAL

The intimate and equal marriage is within the grasp of those who desire it and has been painstakingly laid out in the preceding chapters. The purpose of this chapter is to put in outline form what has been developed one piece at a time, to highlight the cyclical nature of relationship evolution as lived out by couples, and to demonstrate through examples how couples can grow by working through even the most intense struggles.

Our task is not easy because "growing" is not logical and does not lend itself well to outline form. Also, by outlining and labeling a process, we risk diminishing the transformative power embedded in the work.

Discussing the maturing work we generalize under the heading "growth" may be helpful. The kind of maturation that leads men and women to be able to share intimately and equally with each other is felt in rare moments as awesome. During these times, tears of grace abound and partners often shake their heads in disbelief. They still brush their teeth every morning and speak the same language as before (sort of); but what they now know, individually, is so different and so far beyond anything they expected that the joy has no commonly defined word. This growth may happen within a good marriage, as the result of a failed marriage, or within an individual whose marriage is in transition well *before* the marital unit can reflect the growth. Growth can emerge even if the marriage per se can never reflect the growth through mutuality. Like the seed planted in the winter which pushes to the surface in the spring, the shoots will sprout through cracks in concrete if they have to, when the time is right and the person is ready.

The growth in question is a new experience of loving. Most people, when they choose to stay with the process described in previous chapters, hope to fight less, listen longer, feel heard, and gain valuable ground in what is

130

important to them with a partner. They probably will benefit in those ways. Yet, there is much more. Love is maturing from a focus on feelings to a focus on action.

A personal triumph is realized in being able to love another more fully than one knew one could love. The process of going through the seemingly unending cycle: *Choosing* to be vulnerable, *choosing* to deal with conflict, *choosing* to recognize the other whether one agrees with him/her or not, and *choosing* to stay present to self and another through it all, gives people the experience of a lifetime. Many discover their capacity to experience love is greater than they ever dreamed possible.

Years of protecting the self from hurt in hundreds of automatic defensive ways creates a film which surrounds the heart and limits the satisfactions of love. Greater love is longed for, waited for, hoped for in each new romance, but is elusive as long as the person retreats from the threshold of intimacy. Here, during such an unsuspecting time (i.e., smack dab in the middle of painful struggles), the capacity to participate in satisfying love breaks through the film, transforming the persons forever with a step across the threshold. The person now knows he/she is really capable of love, whether or not the current relationship grows or dissolves.

The crystallization of one's capacity to love, which can happen at any time in the cycle, makes earlier love experiences pale in comparison. The transformation at work lifts one out of the familiar and mundane into a connection with God. Every time people become more than they were before, they reach into the spiritual world. They experience the Divine growing in them while still in corporal bodies. In this sacred space, there is often a temporary heightened awareness, which removes scales from the eyes and so captures a person's spirit that he/she can never really enjoy again less than they now know is possible. The awareness empowers one member of a couple, and then hopefully the other, to trust the process, endure the bleak and empty moments, and stay open to the "not-yetness" of their mutual loving until their individual work leads them to another communal spot. In a brush with the Infinite, many find what their souls long for but cannot name until they experience it.

Until this moment, couples have depleted themselves in fruitless efforts to prepackage love. Finally now, they become intimate and equal by totally relinquishing power over the other's journey. Then, they are surprised to find deep within their own beings the love they have sought as an unsuspecting gift.

CYCLE OF GROWTH

The cycle of growth moves clockwise. As a couple's range of love expands, the love-feelings return for a while. At some point, because two selves must be respected and will always differ some, conflict will erupt, again diminishing the love-feelings. The cycle continues in a similar fashion as the first time, with some changes. As one passes the original starting point, one does so from a brand new place on the loop. One has expanded some; one knows more; one brings more to the next revolution. With each new revolution, the cumulative effect results in the person bringing more hope in the process to the choices, less fear, and greater expectations for successful negotiating. The fruits of transformation appear along the way.

THE CYCLE

Love-feelings diminish; they were not really
focused on the other, anyway . . .
Falling-out-of-love-feelings emerge and feel
awful . . .
Estrangement sets in; lovers pull back and wait . .
Disillusionment results from waiting and
measuring the other's love . . .
Forsakenness feelings break the remaining bond.
Standing alone, when they want to run, opens a
new door . . .
Alone Together becomes the first sign of hope. . .
Acknowledgment of the other's needs, and good
intentions begins . . .
Redecision now focuses on honoring the self and

THE CYCLICAL PROCESS

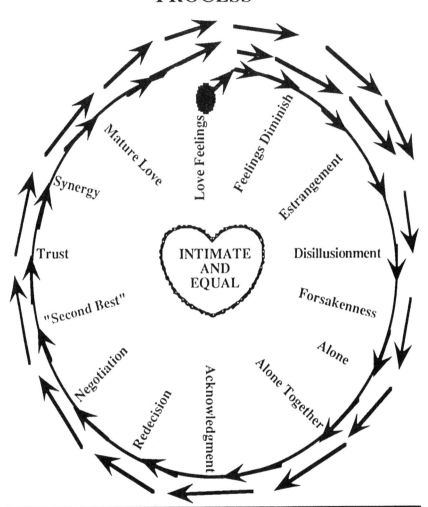

The cyclical process is unending, It begins with love-feelings, progresses through the various stages, resulting in mature love. With mature love, love-feelings return once more, and the cycle begins anew. Eventually the love-feelings diminish, and the ensuing stages are experienced once again, resulting in mature love again. The cycle continues throughout the life of the relationship, each time easier, less painful, less traumatic.

LOVEWORKS

the other in any decision . . .

Learning to Negotiate for mutual satisfaction
enters the story . . .

Finding "Second Best," the first best for the
couple, is a challenge . . .

Trust grows!

The Relationship Synergy changes the dynamics altogether . . .

Mature Love sees, understands, and appreciates
the other . . .

Love-feelings return, but the couple has changed,
so the feelings encompass more than before.

Events or actions intrude on the good feelings . .

AND THE CYCLE CONTINUES . . .

Love-feelings diminish . . .

Falling-out-of-love-feelings are a temptation
again . . .

Estrangement can sneak in when the couple is not
on guard . . .

Disillusionment is an option . . . again! And so
forth as the cycle continues . . .

WHY WOULD ANYONE
ENDURE SUCH TEDIUM ANYWAY?

Why cannot men and women experience the love
they long for and return that love without all this work? We
will address two parts of the question here.

First, greater intimacy demands a larger self to share.
The self can only expand when emotionally separated from
the other, in much the same way a seed must be separated
from its host plant. The formation of males and females
brings gifts and challenges from the family of origin. The
family may or may not provide a safe enough place to grow,
give material luxuries, center a person in spiritual and moral
values, and nurture individual talents. In every case, no one
receives *all* he/she needs by the leaving-home time. One's
potential is rooted; the qualities and skills are probably
formed; yet, every person must stretch into the fullness of

who he/she is . . . alone. Standing alone in the incompleteness of self is what many people try to defy (often, by marrying!) Standing alone cannot be avoided. Only here can people learn what family cannot teach. This is the journey dramatized on the preceding pages: the journey towards a whole self to become free to see and embrace another. When there is more of a person, there is more to share. This is why one might choose to enter the cycle.

Secondly, the structure of marriage, which the Twentieth Century has inherited from its ancestors, is unable to contain two whole selves, intimately and equally connected. Two whole selves were not necessary for marriage to work just two generations earlier. The "complimentary role marriage" successfully utilized two half-evolved selves to meet the expectations and survival needs of marriage. The two halves made a functional whole. But today, because each partner seeks expansion, there is an undeniable yearning to become more complete within oneself, i.e., whole.

Today's "super couples" are limited by a functional marriage of two complimentary halves. Initially, from their complimentary perspectives, men and women are enticed by certain qualities of the other, and dependency develops within this complimentary arrangement. Each lives off the other's half. However, as growth naturally unfolds for each partner, this dependency, which has been the status quo, is now threatened. Partners become very uncomfortable!

The complimentary marriage contract implied: "I'll take care of you and you will take care of me," with each taking responsibility for the other's well-being, fostering dependency. Today, however, our culture's values, time, economic pressures, and a drive for personal fulfillment destabilize the system. The newlywed male who wants to "love" his wife by keeping her from working is devastated by a wife who finds his efforts more controlling than loving. The father who wants to be emotionally involved with the children threatens a woman's traditional field of influence. Each partner's area of growth threatens the other.

The still evolving and expanding marriage needs statements like: "I will look after myself because I know best what I want and need; I will respect your need to do the same. I will also do my best to look after you and your well-being; I will respect and nurture your growth and maturation as well as my own. Together we will cooperate to decide what is best for us jointly." The central issue in the evolution of modern marriage requires acceptance of the inevitable conflict generated by one person's growth infringing upon the other's security.

Personal evolution continues to force marriage, as the chosen home for shared love, to evolve. Just as people cannot change family, government or church without changing their relationship to these institutions, partners cannot change marriage without also changing themselves enormously in the process.

A marriage today will end if it cannot contain evolving men and women, two emerging whole individuals; or worse, the love will die from overcrowding if the marriage notion does not expand. But love is so vital to the human experience, men and women will search for its realization at any cost. Couples will attempt to create new structures to contain the love they want to realize.

Current society evidences the struggles of men and women who cannot find what they need in the old marriage structure and do not yet know the formula for creating the new; hence, the variations of "traditional marriage," "open marriage," "living together," "fear of marriage," "denouncement of marriage," "legally separated marriage" and "divorce." Some "retreat to the old marriage," knowing intuitively that what they see in society today cannot endure for long. It simply does not meet their need.

Two larger, more complete individuals will bring twice the demands, twice the pain, but also double the rewards. As some men and women stretch over the rainbow to find a new kind of marriage, they discover more than they bargained for: They become whole. They search for marriage and find a part of themselves they did not know existed. This permanent gift makes all the difference. Men and women will seek marriage again as the container for love as they now desire it, and marriage cannot help but be trans-

135

formed in the process, too. This is grace at work.

THE ADVANTAGES OF BECOMING
INTIMATE AND EQUAL

With every pass through the cyclical steps:

*   The **interaction becomes** increasingly **less intense**; the stakes are not as high the more couples negotiate through problems.
*   The **potential for resolution** of conflict is **recognized** more **quickly** as couples become facile with this process. They do not sink as deeply into despair and forsakenness as when the only goal was to reestablish love-feelings.
*   **Expectations change** from anticipating a bloody fight to expecting resolution.
*   **Empowered people** communicate better because they are not threatened by mis-communication.
*   **Intimacy is enhanced** because there is more to share.
*   **Each feels more valued by the other.**
*   **Respect increases** and has more value than love-feelings ever had on their best day.

Last but not least:
        *   **The emotional upheaval at the point of forsakenness does not last as long as the first time around and old wounds increasingly heal.**

WHY DOES EMOTIONAL
UPHEAVAL NOT LAST AS LONG?

1.   Healing of wounds from the family of origin is ongoing.

2.   The perceived willingness to work things out

136

lightens the grip on one's old indispensable items.
They are not as big or as important as before because
the feared consequences do not follow.

3.　　Each person knows from standing alone that
the other cannot eradicate their self-value. When the
self is not automatically diminished in conflict, each
can engage the problem sooner with less perceived
risk.

4.　　No one has to retreat from the relationship to
protect self. Each can stand still and hear what is
being said.

5.　　Each now knows the other will at least listen
as best as possible to him/her. This has enormous
power for defusing angry and hurt feelings.

6.　　With expected understanding, each is freer to
consider critical points and express them concisely.

7.　　When agreement with the other's point of
view is no longer necessary to resolve conflict,
acknowledging the other becomes logical, loving,
and easy, and is something anyone can do even if
they are diametrically opposed to the other's plan.

8.　　The relationship is no longer in question,
only finding common ground for resolution.

The Intimate and Equal Relationship includes:

**FORSAKENNESS
ACKNOWLEDGMENT
REDECISION
"SECOND BEST"
NEGOTIATING LOVE
RELATIONSHIP SYNERGY
MATURE LOVE**

A CYCLICAL PROCESS
To weave all these pieces of this complex process together, it is helpful to review the critical steps along the way. Some elements require ongoing reflection to enhance understanding. Some people have asked, "Now, why do I have to teach my partner how to love me? Tell me again." Others have said, "Why do I have to give up what I thought marriage was all about and negotiate for 'second best?' Tell me again. This process seemed right for a while and now it does not make sense anymore." And, "How do I get where I'm going? I've done all the right things and I feel lonely, abandoned, and betrayed. Why?" The comments below address these and other questions, offering new insights for these personal and emotionally stripping experiences.

FORSAKENNESS
The experience of being forsaken by one depended upon for love's security sinks people to the depth of an inner hell. The pain is powerful, lonely, interminable, and paralyzing. People sometimes cannot think, cannot work, and often feel very depressed. Life does not go on as usual for people caught in this shaking-of-the-foundations turmoil. Security is threatened; the familiar is distorted; and words do not capture what people are feeling. It is a shock to the system. No one wants to go through this rupturing of the status quo again. When this experience befalls men and women, they realize how strong their attachments have been. We can only ache with them in the moment of their discovery that the chosen other could not protect them.

Marriage is "supposed" to protect them from times like this. Each is sure that if the situation were reversed, they would not be so cruel. The feelings of forsakenness overwhelm people because they are probably facing the unattainability of one of their cherished indispensable ingredients of love. Grieving the loss of this love fantasy prepares people to realize the love that can be found with the other. Forsakenness must be experienced, felt to the max, and endured. It will end. The human body, mind, and spirit will not stay there too long. The feelings will pass because life has a greater pull than death. People will live again, but a part of what they hold sacred will probably die in the process. It is not really sacred, but it feels like it, and the loss is profound.

This is not a step to be taken lightly, ridiculed, or rationalized but a step which needs to be *felt* all the way to the end. When the grieving is complete, even if people do not have words for what they are grieving about, they will know when it has passed. Perhaps, they dress better, walk lighter, call people they have not wanted to talk to for a while, eat more, and the like. "Second best," the new first best for the couple, cannot even be understood, let alone embraced, until the feelings of forsakenness are allowed their span. Remember that the time frame is different for everyone and will always be longer than anticipated.

ACKNOWLEDGMENT

Standing alone in the aftermath of forsakenness, perhaps still in despair, people can glimpse their partners for the first time in many years. The ones they thought were evil, cruel, mean, selfish, controlling and absolutely wrong are also fragile, vulnerable, hurt, alone, and feeling forsaken, too. Both are hurting, and compassion grows. At least this truth can be acknowledged. Both can be seen as they really are rather than as they have been projected to be. They may not agree how they arrived at this point or who was to blame, but they face each other nevertheless. Agreement about the problem, the solution or even about reality is not the goal of an intimate and equal marriage. Understanding and remaining true to one's self, appreciating the good intentions of self and the other, and *dealing* with the other's truth, however, are vital.

REDECISION

The decision is to honor the partner in all decisions, including whether to stay in the relationship or not and whether to find a new basis for the relationship or not. These are not simply cognitive decisions made casually, but decisions most couples had hoped they never would have to make again. The goal is to achieve mutuality based upon shared responsibility for all decisions. The couple must decide to honor each other or not. The decision to honor the other will move both to a fuller life whether or not they remain together. With this commitment, their children will thrive. If they decide not to honor each other, the children will suffer.

Thinking about whether or not to choose to remain with each other once more is terribly threatening. Moreover, the decision is made during a time of emotional strain, impacted by felt betrayal. People are challenged to find an internal vigil light of faith in the union while feeling despair; not an easy task! They faintly realize that they have contributed in some fashion to the impasses with their fusion to some indispensable requirement of love, but all this is not fully clear yet. In this space, they realize they must relinquish that which they thought was indispensable or the marriage will probably end. This is really a forced choice for many. Not until they are somewhat out of their pain can they appreciate how much they smothered their partner.

A decision to rechoose the partner from compassion fosters peace, no matter how uncomfortable it is sometimes. This decision, based on greater maturity (even in taking responsibility for one's contributions to the impasses), provides stability, allowing redecisions again and again. A compassionate decision steadies the partner and fosters better future arguments around all the ensuing "second bests."

"SECOND BEST" . . . THE NEW FIRST BEST

This is, of course, the first choice the couple can agree on together about any issue. It is their lowest common denominator. Individual first bests give way to the couple's first best. This is not *settling for*, *giving in*, or *giving up* but the process of finding the first best mutually acceptable option. Even a second option may not be feasible, but this only challenges the couple to continue to search for alternatives agreeable to both, no matter how long it takes.

The surprise gift in this sometimes tedious process is the experience of being honored by a partner. It is affirming to know that one will not be usurped by someone else's design. The plans, or needs, or desires of both are equally important. Feeling honored has staying power and allows partners to trust each other to seek resolution, as well as deepening respect for the other and sparking love-feelings.

Many couples, negotiating from places of distrust and *exclusive* self-interest, anticipate being discounted and act according to their natures to protect themselves. For these couples, blame, anger, hurt, and demanding one's way dominate the dialogue.

Couples are surprised by the new first choice negotiation process and feel empowered and hopeful early on, even if there are many arguments. They know that each will give the other all the time needed to reach a mutually satisfactory decision.

NEGOTIATING AS A WAY OF LIFE

Face the truth! Negotiating continues for the life of the relationship. The process is thwarted if either partner takes the attitude: *"If* you do your part, *then* I will do mine." Fulfilling promises is in each person's own best interest. Negotiating for the new first best honors the self as well as the partner and reestablishes credibility, self-esteem, and integrity. Negotiating is exhausting and confusing at first. Partners cannot think clearly; each pounces on any misplaced word; both feel like they are in a fish bowl. The language feels stilted and awkward. Wading through an issue which seemed so simple before it was spoken out loud sets off its own set of firecrackers. Becoming equal is not easy, but so very worth it in the end.

Negotiating is a complex process. Impasses do not necessarily blame anyone but may indicate that one person is still too angry to see a new option, in which case he/she still needs to be acknowledged before anything else can happen. To go back and find a spouse's feelings with them and listen until they feel heard may take time but lays the groundwork for good negotiating. The most difficult task is to stay in one's own space and trust the other is doing the same. Avoid the temptation to conclude the partner is playing mind games.

The process will move along only as fast as the slowest participant. Reaching a resolution will become easier with practice. Resolution will not occur if one feels violated or if one dominates the other. To the degree that each person honors him/herself (by not agreeing to anything that does not seem right) and is willing to deal with the others' reality, no matter how it is construed, negotiating will succeed.

RELATIONSHIP SYNERGY

Relationship synergy is the result of continued interactions making each of the parties more or less predictable to the other. Over time, the relationship becomes more trusted and more intimate. Trust emerges when actual behaviors correspond to promised behaviors. Since trust was broken during the forsakenness time, trust must now be rebuilt one tender step at a time. Trust is not a light switch which is either on or off but more like a dimmer switch, gradually turned brighter or softer. Only on rare occasions is the switch turned off completely or illuminated abruptly.

Because an intimate relationship is an unfolding process rather than an event, if one or the other violates their promised behavior, trust will be diminished. Retrenching is required. The diminished trust level can only be corrected by successfully completing several newly created contracts. Trust will reemerge. The process is fluid: up, down, forward, back, slow, fast, depending on the emotional state of the partners. Note that confidence is building *in the process going on between them* rather than in each other.

As the couple's process unfolds, *belief* is added to the feelings of love and increased understanding of the other. Believing in another *and* the process between them provides the most solid base for a relationship. The intimate and equal marriage is grounded in believing in one's soul that the other can be counted on to work things out, no matter what. As fertilizer for good love, there is none better. A secure relationship can be built upon this foundation. This belief releases an enormous amount of love energy, more than either partner brings by themselves.

142

INTIMATE AND EQUAL: MATURE LOVE

Mature love exists when the well-being of both partners is equally important. Love does not exist on this plane if one partner places his/her well-being either above or below the other. The series of negotiations, resulting in mutually acceptable agreements, increases trust and respect and creates a new basis for loving another. Believing in a process which has more holding power than either partner can sustain alone provides the framework for a new, more mature relationship. People mature; intimacy is understood and shared on a higher plane.

Mature love rekindles the long-lost appreciation of each other. When each partner experiences the mutual fulfillment of promises made during a vulnerable time, profound feelings of love abound again. Infatuation returns, enriched by maturity.

A CYCLICAL PROCESS

An intimate and equal marriage rarely proceeds in an orderly step-by-step manner. Learning new behaviors at an older age, when everyone has so much to unlearn, can be tedious. Sometimes the mistakes are obvious and easily correctable; sometimes not. Couples may handle a difficult situation well one time, only to feel bruised and not considered by the other the very next week. Feelings of forsakenness and the need for acknowledgment of self and the other's pain are paramount, taking precedence over everything because nothing happens until feelings stabilize.

Sometimes, failure to reach early resolution feels like failure of the whole process, ushering in despair and a belief that one has to go back to the beginning. The failure and despair feelings are the products of thinking that this is a linear process. The process is not linear but cyclical, progressive and endless. When a couple returns to the original step they are not quite on the original starting line. The couple is beyond when they first felt love-feelings and became mesmerized by them. They will feel them again and, at some

LOVEWORKS

point, will reach a new impasse which will lead to the need for negotiating another "second best." This will lead to an ever new and even deeper experience of love-feelings. The possibilities in loving are endless.

Remember that understanding the process itself is not enough but must be experienced over . . . and over . . . and over. Conflict and the need to find common denominators present themselves as challenges to be resolved. The temptation exists to think that, finally, conflict will end. No! Conflict will not end, but instead of being so exhausting and tedious as before, it may well become normal and enriching.

The process goes on forever, perhaps never reaching its ultimate goal. But reaching an ultimate goal is not what counts. *Living out the process is what is important!* Marriage is not an event, but a day in and day out process. Consider the following sequence of experiences:

*Conflict is inevitable when there are two different people with different values, dreams, limitations, and strengths. The closer the proximity, the greater the potential for conflict. Conflict becomes the fuel for intimacy in the coming decades.

*Often conflict diminishes love-feelings, and lovers feel alone.

*Standing alone, people wrestle with their own limits and strengths and agonize their way into choices for self-care. Knowing how and being willing to make choices are fundamental qualities for equal partnership.

*Equality in marriage necessitates negotiating mutually acceptable options.

*Mutual solutions demand personal honesty about one's own concerns.

*Mutuality on this plane is the doorway to an intimacy rooted in two whole selves.

*Two whole selves experience greater intimacy and a diminished impact of conflict.

*In an atmosphere of diminished conflict and expanded intimacy, the giving and receiving of love is optimized!

To reinforce the cyclical and sequential nature of this

144

process, this chapter ends with a story of a couple who never expected to find the love they desired with each other. Mike and Marie almost separated three times before they discovered how to be intimate and equal partners.

MIKE AND MARIE:
THE CYCLICAL PROCESS IN MOTION

Mike and Marie met and married young. She came from a very well known and economically established family where the maternal grandfather was the powerful patriarch. Marie's mother and father divorced when she was very young, expanding her grandfather's influence into their daily choices. Mike came from a family with less community prestige. His father established his own economic success, although he controlled everything in his path to make it happen. Mike's parents are still together.

This couple began married life on a giant success wave created by their families. Later, business losses in both families affected them directly. Money became tight, fear set in, and personal insecurity interfered with loving.

Marie, when insecure and feeling controlled by forces outside herself, would rebel, drink too much, stay out late, and keep secrets. Most of all, she would overeat and then take diet pills. Growing up, Marie rarely had opportunities to feel powerful and in charge of her own life. She often felt controlled and naturally transferred these feelings to Mike and his family. She perceived Mike as controlling when he questioned her.

Mike, the son of a dominant father and passive mother, hated arguing; he tended to hide his massive internal anxiety with external compliancy. At one point, a business venture with his father failed, draining the family savings. Then, he managed a wholesale business as his main source of income. Although officially retired, Mike's father co-owned the business and continued to give Mike orders. Mike often had trouble trusting his own judgment and making decisions, feeling guilty when confronting his father and inadequate when he did not. Depression resulted from the insecurity he felt in stepping away from his father and making the business the way he wanted it to be.

145

LOVEWORKS

1. Love-feelings diminish: Shortly, the couple, who had not completed their separation-from-family work, began to evidence stress. They did not like each other's ways. They readily saw the other's foibles and authoritatively reported them. Love-feelings diminished as each needed to defend oneself against the other more often. Both expected the other to change.

2. Falling-out-of-love-feelings prevail: Mike and Marie had an uncanny ability to be quite rational, quiet, and even respectful, no matter how angry, upset, or abused each felt. Well versed in good communication skills, they listened well and were clear in presenting their facts. However, they still could not share their deeper truths. That would come later.

3. Estrangement: They lived in the non-love-feeling state for quite a while: Marie, over consuming food and diet pills; Mike, depressed and avoiding decisions while trying to act like he was in charge. They became pregnant, felt some renewed hope and a spark of love for each other, and prepared for parenthood. Mike rallied in the business, while Marie settled down to become the best mother ever. At least, she could have some control over her own children.

4. Disillusionment: Disagreements about how to raise the child, the older generation confounding them with every decision, several years of low income from the business, the death of Marie's grandfather, and clinical depression overcoming Mike brought severe disillusionment to this couple. They supported a huge home with diminishing savings from the one-time windfall and paid out a mammoth monthly debt. He focused on her frivolous spending, lack of support for his efforts, immaturity, laziness, lack of concern for him, and her addiction. She focused on his depression, controlling family, lack of love for her, and minimal help at home. The more he pulled, the more she pushed away, and vice versa. The marriage was threadbare.

5. Forsakenness: Each felt abandoned, alone, unloved, and trapped. Each knew what the other should do to repair the brokenness and felt angry that they did nothing. Both felt they were singularly working at the relationship and making compromises. Mike's depression deepened, and he worked less. Marie did creative things with her son, decorated tee shirts late into the evening to sell at the flea market, and continued to distance herself from Mike. She consumed the diet pills surreptitiously and planned to leave Mike at some point. Marie felt unloved and fully responsible now that Mike was ill. She would no longer walk on egg-shells just because he acted depressed.

Mike hoped the shell of manhood he put forth would suffice. He was terrified; it was difficult to get out of bed in the morning or go to sleep at night. When he worked, he pretended well enough, then hid in his office and napped. Shame permeated his being. Mike hated himself and all those around him. When he could barely move, Marie chastised him for not playing with their child. He screamed out to her from inside his head, but, of course, the sounds never left his lips.

6. Standing alone . . . the first time: At this point, they were pregnant again and discussed terminating the pregnancy. Pros and cons with quiet poignancy passed back and forth in many exchanges. They chose to keep the child and attempt to build their even more threadbare marriage. Personal disillusionment limited love-feelings, diminishing their capacity to do little more than merely exist with each other for quite a while. They were tending to their own needs now, feeling badly that the other would not change.

7. Alone . . . together: Mike and Marie began to recognize that each had the same kind of pain and to hear the other's way of thinking. They agreed not to see each other as an enemy and began to believe the other had good intentions. When extended family tried to "parent" contrary to the couple's chosen style, they stood united. The couple could agree for the children's sake and support each other. Yet, confronting the extended family took its toll. To disagree with the God-like commands from on high was personally challenging and maritally rewarding and bore fruit.

8. Acknowledgment: Compassion grew as they recognized how difficult it was to confront either family. This compassion extended to other issues. Marie began to

147

understand Mike's depression and his perception that she was usurping his authority in his own home. She did not agree with him but understood. Mike appreciated Marie's need to participate in decision making and her resentment when he would dictate how things should be at home or how money should be spent. She understood his hesitancy to be authoritative at work; maybe he compensated by devaluing and discrediting her at home. Mike heard Marie this time when she verbalized her hurts and concerns.

9. Redecision: The couple began to talk more respectfully now, hearing more than they had in the past. They realized each was offended by the other's actions. Even the simplest situations had been interpreted by the outsider's eye as negative. They decided to give each other another chance.

10. Negotiating: With shared honesty, Mike began to recover. Marie, distanced from Mike, had not left the marriage fully. She had accessed some personal power. While Mike was ill, Marie raised the children. She may have felt lonely and she may have succumbed to her pills, but she held the family together for a very long year. This raised her self-esteem. As Mike grew stronger, Marie offered common sense suggestions for his business. Mike listened to her for the first time, no longer threatened. They mutually agreed about finances, her involvement at the business, his contribution to home maintenance and child care, and dealing with their families. Some issues, however, privately burdened each of them and were never mentioned. Consequently, the marriage was still affected by secrets. They had grown some, but more was to come.

11. "Second Best": "Second best" was not difficult until they totally disagreed with the other's ridiculous logic. Then each reverted to control and guilt tactics, held in abeyance but not forgotten. "Second best" crystallized over where their second child would attend preschool. Marie and Mike faced off here, trying futilely to overpower the other. The impasse threatened the marriage again. All their progress piled like chips on the roulette table, awaiting the roll of the dice. They had inadvertently put their self-value on

148

the table with the decision about the child. Marie had made good decisions for the children's education all along; she wanted to be the authority here. She took her stand around psychological concern for her son's adaptability through an unnecessary change. Mike helped build the new school down the street and negated Marie's concerns after consulting with a counselor. He thought she was being unreasonable, and she thought he was diminishing her authority. The fight was not about the reasonableness of changing schools. The fight was about power and, ultimately, self-esteem. These fights cannot be won with reasonable arguments.

People can become emotionally stringent when they harbor unspoken demands bolstered by emotional issues. A problem may surface which evokes strong emotions, and the issue is soon convoluted. The energy surge does, however, testify to deeper level dis-ease. While deciding "your way, my way, or no way," as they tugged at their son from opposite directions, Mike and Marie faced the "if you really loved me, you would" issue in their hearts. Yet, with extreme difficulty they mutually resolved the school issue and redressed their self-value issues separately.

12. Trust: Mike asked Marie one day why she was not warm toward him. She was open to him sometimes, but often she would give him the cold shoulder. He found her to be a cold person and was disturbed by her criticism. Now she mostly avoided him. He needed to feel loved and questioned her love for him. Marie responded honestly, revealing her conviction that he did not even *like* her. She felt he had rebuffed her suggestions for improving business, for investing money, for entertaining parents, and many other things over the years. Marie believed he tolerated her ways but had little respect for her talents. She resented his constant questioning about everything she did.

When she said she was sure he did not like her very much, his heart flooded with feeling, and his truth poured out, too. Mike was dumbfounded, having no idea she received him as devaluing her. He had another reason for scrutinizing her. Now it was his turn to tell her a private truth of his own. He risked telling her that he thought she was still taking pills. That was why he was skeptical and watched her so carefully. He hated her moodiness and brittle nature when on the pills. He watched her crash and then be on a high, sometimes cleaning floors at three in the morning. Mike was never certain if Marie was on pills or just grumpy. She looked at him open mouthed. "Do you mean, you have been watching me like a hawk because you think I am taking pills? I thought it was because you thought I was incompetent." Surprise and relief settled in.

13. Synergy: This was the beginning of a new openness between them. Neither intended to hurt or devalue the other; yet, each was hurt and devalued. Revealing their secrets released more energy than either of them had and opened the possibility of more shared truths. Even in the decision to give each other a new chance, they had protected vulnerable places.

14. Return of love-feelings: They smiled more at each other. Feelings long forgotten commanded them to touch more, call more from work, respond to the other's presence more. Something had been missing; neither knew what it was. Life had gotten so much better when they learned to negotiate, but now it was even better.

Today, eight years into the process of marrying, they feel intimate with each other for the first time. The love-feelings do not feel like they did when the couple was younger. They have been through much, respected each other enough not to destroy each other, and created the way for more truth to draw them closer together. Mature love blossomed. Mature love is the unmistakable realization that they are putting each other's well-being on the same level via the whole process as experienced over and over again. Then love-feelings return.

1. Love-feelings on a mature plane satisfy them for a while . . . until an unexpected impasse again invites them to struggle through all the steps . . . again and again and again!!

CHAPTER 13
ABUNDANT FRUIT

THE PROGRESSIVELY ENLARGING CYCLE

As we indicated in the last chapter, the life cycle of a relationship is ongoing and progressively enlarging. With each pass around the starting point, the partners are brought to their knees, then reestablished, and eventually reconciled. The process transforms them individually. They mature emotionally and deepen spiritually.

When the partners exhaust their personal resources on the unrealizable quest for perfect love, they come to appreciate the Grace bestowed upon them. Despite their thwarted efforts, they are loved, but this time by a love that is not as familiar or well known; it has not been earned or deserved. Love enters by admitting defeat, surrendering to the flow, and gathering the remains. You may ask if this love is a gift or a choice. It is both.

Choosing to love from inner security, not marital security, is somewhat rational, often intuitive and embedded in emotional collapse. There remains the ever present invitation to destroy the other before they can destroy one's self or accept the other in the mutuality of psychic pain. Each must choose between life and death. The choice at this point is crucial!

This process has been well articulated in many books, philosophies, and religions around the world. It is not a new concept. For that very reason we suggest the cyclical process between men and women today is a profound microcosm of life that leads people to the Divine.

Both authors were raised in homes which used the phrase, "God is Love," but not until recently has the meaning of the phrase been understood in the "troubles" of men and women. The "war between the sexes" is also the birthplace of love, love that transcends one's abilities. One has only to choose life, not death; stand still, not run away; give up the quest, not perish defending one's rights. In this sense, the troubles themselves are the vehicle to the Divine.

Perhaps this is the reason for the man/woman predicament, to lead them into the Love of God with each other.

The problem in loving is *supposed* to be there! Now the answer to the question about divorces set forth at the beginning of this book is clear. There are so many divorces because struggling couples are dealing with the human condition at its most primitive level. A simple example emerges in the gender stereotype for sexual enjoyment we noted in an earlier chapter: Women want or need emotional intimacy to enjoy sex; men want or need to have sex in order to be emotionally intimate. This uncovers a root problem, especially now that intimacy is the goal and equality is the means to that end. Neither of the sexes is entitled to have their needs met at the expense of the other, creating a standoff. This most human impasse can destroy the couple or, with the help of faith and belief, can make them more God-like in their loving. All backbreaking impasses wear couples out. Friends and relatives wear out, too. It is deceptively freeing to label the other, to raise oneself above the other, to devalue the other, and wrongfully to represent the other in the name of putting some period to endless arguing. Such actions are fruitless. All couples, even in their worn out shoes, have the challenge to choose life over death. Yet, this decision remains a choice.

THE COUPLE

Remaining together or not is not indicative of life (love) or death (hate). Some couples remain together, killing each other daily. Others sadly divorce, yet love daily in mutual respect by living and letting live. The choice between life or death remains an option every day no matter the arrangement between the partners. As long as husbands and wives, or former spouses, choose life over death they will live love which has transformative power. This energy can give life to any arrangement.

Since the particular composition between men and women matters less, the stage is set to look more constructively at how our society can function even though families differ structurally. If the family is considered the building

152

block of the society, then the marital bond is the cornerstone of the family. When spouses and former spouses live this kind of love by placing the well-being of the other at the same level as one's own, there is a foundation for relationship, a family, a community, a society, a nation, and a world of nations. Male/female relational problems are really a microcosm of the problems of the world; therefore, the resolutions to larger problems are also strikingly similar to the solutions for men and women in their intimate relationships. Consider these spheres that contain the same dynamic.

THE FAMILY

Yes, the North American family truly is in trouble, mostly because the parents are at war, fighting about whose ideas of love will take precedence. The children become refugees. They have no shelter, no means of emotional support, and are without a peaceful home. Most children hold on miraculously well while the parents struggle with each other. But when war is the option of choice, the children grow up in an emotional war zone. They learn how to kill rather than be killed. Life is diminished, holding little meaning, and nothing but the moment has any value.

Since the mothers and fathers are so caught up with their interpersonal struggle, the children have precious little of their parents' time and attention. From necessity, their identities as young men and women come less from the parents and more from the peer group of other refugees or from the television. Both are far less than optimal. Can we fault young men and women for being angry, demoralized, and cynical when the mothers and fathers they know cannot circumvent their troubles with each other?

On the other hand, when children witness their parents making peace with a mutually acceptable armistice, they will become the children of parents who believe in and live love, even if not together under the same roof. This model of love demonstrated daily will sustain them and give them something to live for, some hope, something real.

People used to say that couples would "stay together for the children." Now we say couples must *resolve* their relationships for the children, but this does not necessarily house them under the same roof. They must devote themselves to the needs of the family until the children are grown, whether or not they live together. In so doing, they communicate honor and respect for this family, even though they may have new love partners.

This kind of love does not come from the television but is rooted daily in the choice of life over death, in love over hate, in reconciliation over derision. Even in the most difficult blended family, the children can see their biological parents cooperating, making mutually acceptable decisions about their children's lives. Since there is no war and, therefore, no real danger, loyalty issues are minimal and the parents are available to the children!

Pursuits other than survival become possible for these children. Children and parents can now participate in the community and enjoy productive lives.

THE COMMUNITY

In North America we live under the ethos of winning. This is a direct reflection of the male orientation to life and is what we would expect when community events are heavily influenced by masculine traits. Therefore, community problems are dominated by position-taking, sabre rattling, and advocacy for the self-righteous interests of one group over the other. The results are the diminishing of others along with their values, and less tolerance of diversity in general. Wars abound between conservative and liberal elements, in churches, on school boards, in neighborhoods, on boards of directors of social agencies, and in local governments. The problems in these groups contain the same dynamics experienced by men and women seeking their loves.

In many cases our communities have become as paralyzed as our marriages. Advocacy for both legal and social rights cannot solve problems without cultivating retribution and revenge or demoralization of the losers. When part of a school board politically outmaneuvers the minority, the seeds of counteractive forces are sown, which at the next election reverse the field. Teachers, students, and parents become refugees feeling ill-served by the very organization which is supposed to give them direction and security. The public concludes nothing can be done about problems that continue to plague daily life.

All parties to community decision making have ideas on how things should be. In pursuit of the utopia, they negate the best assets of each other in much the same way couples do when they seek the love held in their own heads. Not getting what they want is threatening. People think that something indispensable will have to be relinquished in order to reach accord with the other side! Trying to convince the other side to see the truth or righteousness of a position inflames the situation rather than resolves the issue. On the brink of disaster the parties have a decision to make. Do they wish to destroy the other side or find a way to work this out in some mutually acceptable manner? Whether they go their own ways or not, will they be reconciled in the process or continue to fan flames of anger supported by claims of self-righteousness? All communities, the church, the school, the corporation, the hospital, the nonprofit agency, the club, the local government all mirror the problems between men and women.

THE SOCIETY

Race relations, as well as public issues like abortion, medical intervention, health insurance, etc. all face the same challenge. Good men and women can destroy each other in the process or find ways to identify common values around which they can cooperate for "second best." If a minority feels prejudice from an employer, or a woman feels sexually harassed, or a patient feels mistreated by a physician, would it not be far better to find out from the oppressed how to address the feelings of prejudice in a mutually acceptable manner? Doing so would speak louder than subjectively defined good and noble intentions. We only have to be willing to learn a little of the other's language to make a big difference and give up on the society we espouse in our own heads.

155

THE GOVERNMENT

Suppose the Democrats and the Republicans gave up trying to convince the other side of the legitimacy of their self-interests and spent more time finding ways to address each other's legitimate needs. Would this not be a more fruitful use of time? We would save billions of dollars normally spent on one study after the other showing how right one side is over the other. We might have to accept the harsh reality that we have to work from both ends if we are really going to deal effectively with our problems. Building more jails *and* moderating the effects of poverty might be our only answer. Yes, the expense will be greater than we thought, but then again, we all might feel better about ourselves and our government. In the long run, it might even be less expensive.

"WE DID NOT START THE FIRE"

A contemporary rock artist, Billy Joel, sang the above line. The video accompanying the piece contained a series of flashes on nodal events over the Twentieth Century. It made a clear statement that our society has been moving along at a tremendous clip and that no one person is responsible, yet we all are responsible because we are part of it. No one woke up one day and said, "Gee, I think it would be a good idea if all women and men were equals," and from that point on went out and started proselytizing everyone. It simply does not work that way. Social movements are a natural part of the evolutionary process: maturation on a grand scale.

There is no question however, that the baby boomers have seized upon the notion with tenacity. Most are in the process of making the necessary changes, others give lip service to the idea, and still others have kept it quiet in their hearts, not wanting to rock the boat. But even for these folks, the notion of equality between the sexes is an unstated awareness which leaks out in their daily living.

A distinct minority of baby boomers have come through the entire process. They are considerably scarred, but would never go back to anything less. These people

156

have risked everything, without models, for an ideal which is scoffed at by most of the world. Even now, these men and women struggle against their own gender to maintain their integrity. The men must defend themselves not only against traditional men who wish to maintain superiority over women but also against more modern men who seem to imply that accepting equality with women undermines some innate quality of being masculine. The women must defend themselves against those who wish to remain secure in their secondary status as a trade-off for security as well as from the jeers of more modern feminists who scoff at a woman who longs to find fulfillment with a man.

We owe a tremendous debt to these people who continue to push forward. They are sprinkled all around. Some are married to the same partner. Some divorce and live alone; others have a second or third partner. Some have never married but have been together for twenty years or more. Some live alone, knowing their capacity to love as an equal even though they do not now enjoy the companionship of an intimate and equal partner. We want to take the time to thank them and encourage them all as they continue to experiment with the frontiers of male/female relationships. They will not stop because they cannot stop. They are drawn to life with others. The fire no one started continues to burn.

THE GRAND CANYON AND
THE COLORADO RIVER

The Grand Canyon is probably the most awesome sight in North America. We are told that the land has risen and the river has worn the gorge and eroded the rock earth. Men and women are like two rims of the canyon having risen out of their respective pasts and been affected by a tremendous social force known now as the river of equality. This social impetus has changed the landscape perhaps forever.

If one stands on the foot bridge at the base of the canyon over the river, one can see a curious aspect of the back washes and whirlpools so strong that white rapids swirl round and round in an upstream direction. Eventually, they merge with the major flow and continue down the river. As in the formation of the walls of the canyon there has been a devastating price created by the rising numbers of men and women who are interested in equality. A great amount of damage has been done to the lives of many other human beings who never asked to be part of a social movement. These people's lives have been shattered and they do not know why.

The children of the baby boomers have paid the worst price of all. Too many have been neglected as the parents have understandably fought to come to terms with what was happening to them. These children suffer in the back wash of the movement. Some of them will move back along the stream, hoping to find more security in the former vertical arrangement between men and women. This is the natural ebb and flow of the river along the canyon.

While we cannot do much for those who have been so hurt and who will still be hurt because of this social movement, we can at least help them understand what this has all been about. For this reason we leave them this manuscript.

> "... the end of all our striving is to arrive at
> the point from which we began, but to know
> the place for the first time."
>
> T. S. Eliot

EPILOGUE
THE TENNIS GAME

Envision with us a game of tennis between a man and a woman. It is a new ball game in which neither sex is better equipped to play than the other. The only catch is that women have been dreaming of this kind of game for a long time. Both have much to learn.

The woman says: "Let me teach you to play a new version of tennis that I have been imagining. I would like to be an equal player with you. This game requires hitting balls back and forth across a net. I know you tend to hit balls hard. Will you consider softening your serve so I can return the ball and keep the volley going? Let's keep the volley going as long as possible instead of trying to defeat each other."

The man says to the woman: "Well, I have never played tennis before. I do not know how to volley, but I'm willing to learn. Physical activities tend to come easily to me. But I'm a little mystified by the goal of this new game; it feels weird. I play games to win. Maintaining a volley is a strange challenge. It has never occurred to me to play a game to sustain a volley. It seems senseless."

So the man agrees to learn tennis with the woman who has been teaching children to play tennis for years. She steps up to the line and hits the first ball over the net to the man. In a flash, she drops her racket, runs like hell over to the other side of the net before the ball drops and stands behind the man. She holds his arm and positions him for a swing in time to hit the ball.

Quickly, she runs across the court back to the other side of the net to return the volley from her side. She discards her racket again on the run back to the man's side for a repeat of the process until she falls flat on her face from exhaustion.

The man is puzzled by the action in this new game, especially because the woman seems agitated. She is exhausted, and he has not even broken a sweat. Somehow this is now his fault! He is mystified by her anger which

159

triggers his anger in return. Was not this her idea to begin with? Feeling blamed for her exhaustion, he threatens to quit. Thinking fast, she devises a new plan. Perhaps she could play tennis on roller skates to ease the trek back and forth across the court. This ploy could eliminate exhaustion and facilitate teaching the man to play the game in a way which would keep her central to the action. Well, skinned knees and new exhaustion do her in this time. Both concur they need to make changes. To play tennis together, he must learn how to hit the ball back to her and modify his competitive attitude. She must stop skating helter-skelter over the court.

She is despondent and he is lost. She says, "I am frustrated being in charge of this new game. But I so genuinely want a new ball game with you, I'll work myself to the bone if I have to so that we can play together." Bewildered, the man looks at her and says, "If you want me in this game, I have to hit the ball myself. I want to be in this game too but I can't play this way. I must start swinging and see what happens. You'll be most helpful to me if you take off the roller skates and stay on your side of the net. Then you can hit the ball when it falls on your side."

The woman is at first quite skeptical of this suggestion. She wonders what tricks he has up his sleeve to sabotage the new game. Does she not know more about this game than he does? She has been imagining it for years! Of course, he'll need more help. But she has to admit that she is tired and would welcome having to do only her part. She smiles at him and says, "Okay, I'll stay on my side of the court, but I'll keep the roller skates on in case you need my help."

The man is glad the net divides them. Maybe now he can figure out this new game. Still confused about the volleying idea, he wonders why one hits a ball just for the sake of returning the ball. It reminds him of playing catch which a guy only does until he can enter the real game. And why does she still want to keep those roller skates around? Does she have something planned for him that he does not know about? Well, he cannot deal with that now. He needs to concentrate on changing all the rules in his head about how to play a game with a woman. He hears himself telling her, "Let's go slowly. If you hit the ball gently to me, I'll try to hit it back to you so that it lands where you are. I know you want a longer volley. Let's see what we can do."

Unbeknownst to him, she breathes a sigh of relief. She was afraid he'd give up and quit. "Sure," she says to him as she prepares herself for a lengthy tennis lesson, a little surprised that he would ask *her* to go slowly to help him out. She thought he could pick up the game quickly if he wanted to. However, the longer they stay on the court, the more likely they are to hit longer volleys which is all she wants anyway. She relaxes a little and takes off the roller skates. When she looks up, he is grinning at her. She shrugs her shoulders and hopes they can have a little fun with this game. He's amazed she does not really believe he wants to learn the game (he does want a good relationship, too). Maybe he should tell her so, soon. On the outside he says, "It will take me some time but I will develop some skill at this sport. I've exhausted my ability and desire to sustain the familiar competitive pace of other sports, anyway."

He looks like he is not going to say anymore, then changes his mind and says, "You seem to have a good idea how this game is supposed to be played, but it might not look like tennis at all when I develop more skills in this game. Right now we'll volley your way but this might become an entirely new game in the future." That seemed like a mouthful for him. He waited to see what she would do with what he said.

She wanted him to know that she really did not like teaching this game and she did not care what kind of a game it turned into so long as he stayed in the game. Having spent far too many years imagining how this new game would feel, she didn't want to impede this opportunity over a technicality.

Putting down her tennis racket, she approached the net. "Neither of us has any idea how this game will evolve, but I for my part will promise to stay on my side of the net, put away my roller skates, and keep my eye on the ball where ever it lands." He jumps in and says, "I can work with you this way. There's still a challenge present, even though the game is no longer about winning and losing. The ball is clearly in my court now." What he does not say out loud is that he is relieved she'll not try to play his game for him. He is a little scared, though, of the demands on him to keep playing, with no end in sight. What will she do if he wants to quit? Maybe sustaining this volley will be harder for him than he thought.

Ninety minutes later the partners stand looking at each other. Sweaty, weary, and happy, they approach the net. She comments in a pleasing tone that he did pretty well. He says that he was surprised how challenging it was to maintain a volley with their different skill levels. They each had compensated a little for the other in different ways.

The woman fantasized about future encounters on the tennis court. She liked what they were doing, felt good about her skill and looked forward to regular afternoons of play with him, maybe even tomorrow. She might even shed a few of those extra pounds. With the woman gazing lovingly at the man, they walked together off the court. He turned to her and said, "Want to take a shower together?"